CONTENTS

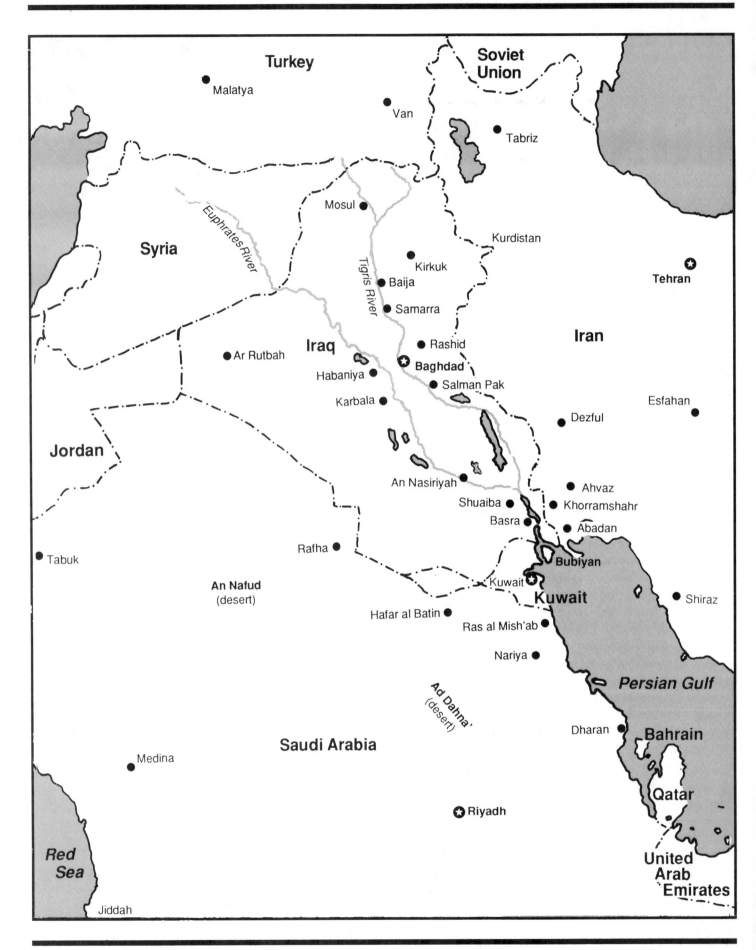

GULF WAR
FACT BOOK™

Frank Chadwick and Matt Caffrey

Copyright©1991 GDW, Inc.
All rights reserved. Made in U.S.A. Printed in U.S.A.
ISBN 1-55878-094-7.

Color maps courtesy of the Defense Mapping Agency
and Her Majesty's Stationery Office.

These charts should not be used for navigation of aircraft.
This product is not officially sponsored or endorsed by the Department of
Defense or the Defense Mapping Agency.

Gulf War Fact Book™ is a trademark name of GDW, Inc.
for its information book about the Persian Gulf War.

Written and Researched By: Frank Chadwick and Matt Caffrey
Additional Research: Loren K. Wiseman
Art Direction: Steve Bryant
Graphic Design and Production: Amy Doubet, LaMont Fullerton, Jeff Kohl,
Keith Ganske, and Eric W. Haddock
Typesetting and Editing: Julia Martin and Stephen Olle
Typing: Elise Ganske, Aaron Ruby, and Jamie Fike

P.O. Box 1646
Bloomington, IL 61702-1646

THE GULF WAR
FOREWORD

Our original book, the **Desert Shield Fact Book**, received an overwhelmingly positive response. The question asked the author, perhaps hundreds of times, was when a follow-up book would appear detailing the history of the war. The answer, of course, is in your hands.

As natural a project as a history of the war seemed, it was undertaken with some trepidation. The original product set a standard of presenting well-researched information in a very easily understood format. Living up to those same standards when writing about a war scarcely over was intimidating.

Fortunately, many people were extremely helpful in assembling this book. Although the front cover lists me, Frank Chadwick, as the author, my coauthor, Matt Caffrey, was equally instrumental in making this book something that both of us could be proud of. Matt brought to the project a knowledge and understanding of air operations that are as essential to its success as they had been to the success of Operation Desert Storm.

The final result is, we believe, the most complete history available on the Gulf War. With the passage of time, more detailed information will no doubt emerge, and some of the smaller battles of the war will be able to be examined in greater detail. In terms of the overall course of the campaign, however, we are confident that the conclusions presented here will endure.

MILITARY AFFAIRS AND YOU

The authors bring to this project a philosophy of military affairs which is worth explaining. Understanding this philosophy will go a long way toward understanding the philosophy of the book.

Americans are not very well versed in military affairs in an absolute sense. How they rank in knowledge versus other nations in unclear. Perhaps everyone in the world is as ignorant or more so than are we. Whether that is true or not, it is certainly true that Americans are, in absolute terms, more ignorant of military affairs than they are of most sporting games.

Why this is the case could be the subject of an interesting discussion someday, but it is beside the point for now. All that is important is that the above statement is true.

It is widely held that the general public knows little about the military because it is too complex a subject for them. This is patently untrue, and the denial of that claim is at the heart of this book. The authors hold that military affairs are well within the grasp of the average person, if clearly communicated. This is so because military science, at its best, is a simple, straightforward, and common-sense approach to achieving political objectives by force. Once that is grasped, everything else falls into place fairly easily.

Rather than talk first about a bewildering array of weapon systems and capabilities, we have instead tried to start with the problems faced by the military. These things, such as distance, darkness, inclement weather, the need to supply troops in forward positions, and so forth, by their very existence suggest possible solutions. In the progressive refinement of those solutions lies the logic of various weapon system capabilities. And it is the *logic* of military affairs that we are most interested in communicating.

HISTORY VERSUS JOURNALISM

Can a book written so soon after an event be history, or is it doomed to be little more than simple reporting? Ultimately, that is for you to decide. However, it is certainly possible to write about the war with historical issues firmly in mind, and that is what we have endeavored to do.

While our primary focus has been on reporting the events of the war, we have tried never to lose sight of the fact that these are not isolated events which sprang spontaneously into being. The type of war fought in the gulf has its roots in the histories of the Coalition armies and the Iraqi Army, and we have tried to make that historical context clear. Certainly an understanding of it makes the events which followed much more understandable.

Not only does the Gulf War have a unique set of historical antecedents, it will also continue to "make history" for some time to come. The world's view of the global military balance, the costs versus gains of aggression, and the options available for applying force and avoiding the application of force, have all be changed profoundly by the Gulf War, and will never be the same again.

The river of history has cut its banks, and is finding a new course. Where this new channel takes us in the years to come will be very interesting.

THE SEEDS OF WAR

The Persian Gulf is the location of some of the world's oldest trade routes. For as long as there have been trade routes, there have been conflicts over them. Likewise, ever since there have been borders, there have been border disputes. Oil is a relatively recent bone of contention, but one of global importance.

Both Iraq and Kuwait were once part of the Ottoman Turkish Empire, which was broken up by the League of Nations after the defeat of the Ottoman Empire during the First World War. Iraq had an ancient tradition of national independence dating back to the time of the Babylonians, but over the centuries had been part of the Persian and Turkish empires. Kuwait was one of a number of small semi-independent emirates ruled by the Ottomans.

The Al-Sabah family founded the emirate of Kuwait in 1759, but the area had been annexed by the British in 1899. The British administered Iraq under a mandate from the League of Nations after WWI. In effect, this made Iraq and Kuwait colonies in all but name: Britain controlled their economy and their diplomatic relations, and was responsible for their defense. The mandate ended in 1932, when a king was installed in Iraq by the British. Kuwait remained a British protectorate until after the Second World War, finally acquiring independence in 1961.

Oil was discovered in the region in the 1930s, but WWII prevented its exploitation until 1946. Both Iraq and Kuwait were founding members of the Organization of Petroleum Exporting Countries (OPEC), a coalition formed to control prices and impose limits on annual production of oil.

IRAQ

Iraq was a viable nation-state before oil. It now has a fair system of agriculture, mineral deposits (in the northern mountains), and some industry. Iraq is almost self-sufficient agriculturally, and its industrial capacity gives it much more economic viability than Kuwait. In many ways, it is a potentially dangerous powerhouse, especially if it continues its alleged nuclear program.

The British-imposed limited monarchy was destroyed with the assassination of King Feisal II in 1958, and a republic was established, but no elections have been held since that time. The present provisional constitution has been in effect since the Ba'ath (renaissance) Socialist Party of Iraq (BPI) overthrew the government of then-Prime Minister Kassem, and took power in 1968. Saddam Hussein, the current president, was an important member of the BPI since 1959, and held several important government positions from 1968 onward, becoming president after disposing of his rivals in 1979.

Iraq has had border conflicts of varying intensity with almost all of its neighbors since the end of the mandate, ranging from diplomatic notes exchanged with Syria to the Iran-Iraq War. Iraqi troops even entered Kuwait briefly in 1973.

KUWAIT

Kuwait has effectively no resources besides oil: Most of the land is arid desert, and the country depends upon foreign imports for all of its food and some of its drinking water. Ninety percent of Kuwait's export income is from petroleum and petroleum products, the remainder is largely from re-exports.

Kuwait attained its independence from Britain in 1961, when the United Kingdom largely withdrew its influence from the Persian Gulf. It has been ruled by the Al-Sabah emirs, under a constitution adopted in 1963 (although certain electoral provisions were suspended in 1976) since that time.

ORIGINS OF THE CONFLICT

The origins of the Iraq-Kuwait conflict go back generations. Many of the borders in the region were arbitrarily imposed by the British during the 1930s. A major point of continual conflict has been the large Rumaila oil field, which straddles the Iraq-Kuwait border.

Basically, Iraq claims that Kuwait has been pumping more oil from the Rumaila field than it is entitled to. Iraq claims that Kuwait ignored OPEC production ceilings in the late 1980s, selling more than its quota on the open market, and consequently costing Iraq millions in lost revenue. Also, Iraq claims that Kuwait was once part of the old Ottoman province of Basra, and that during the Ottoman Empire and continuing under the British mandate both Iraq and Kuwait were administered from Baghdad. Thus, Kuwait should rightfully have been made a part of Iraq in 1932, with the establishment of the present Iraqi state.

Further points of contention are Warba and Bubiyan islands, which block direct access to the Iraqi port of Umm Qasr from the Persian Gulf. Iraqi-bound oil tankers must pass through the narrow confines off these islands, and their possession by another nation was a continuing irritant to Iraq.

Finally, in 1990, Iraq demanded that Kuwait cede its portion of the Rumaila field to Iraq, and demanded $2.5 billion in reparations for the oil removed from it illegally, as well as another $14 billion in lost Iraqi revenue due to quota violations. Iraq also demanded cancellation of $12 billion in loans made by Kuwait to Iraq during the Iran-Iraq War. The Kuwaitis refused to discuss the matter, and Iraq began massing troops in July as a means of forcing Kuwait to the negotiation table.

As it turned out, the negotiations

lasted less than an hour. Many observers believe that Iraqi demands were set excessively high to provide a premise for an invasion. Certainly Iraq was facing an economic catastrophe. The war with Iran and the military buildup which followed had left the country mired in debt. Iraq's GDP (Gross Domestic Product) had been about $45 billion in 1988, while its national debt had skyrocketted to $80 billion. The decline in world oil prices sent government revenues plunging, and left it with no real means for recovering from its debt burden.

No means save one. Invasion of Kuwait would immediately wipe out a large portion of Iraq's debts. Looting the Kuwaiti treasury would provide needed hard currency to keep the economy running. And control of the Kuwaiti oil fields would not only give Iraq access to larger oil revenues in a gross sense, it would also give it greater controls over supply and, thus, final market price.

GULF WAR
FACT BOOK
The Seeds of War

On August 2, spearheaded by the Republican Guard Corps, the Iraqis struck.

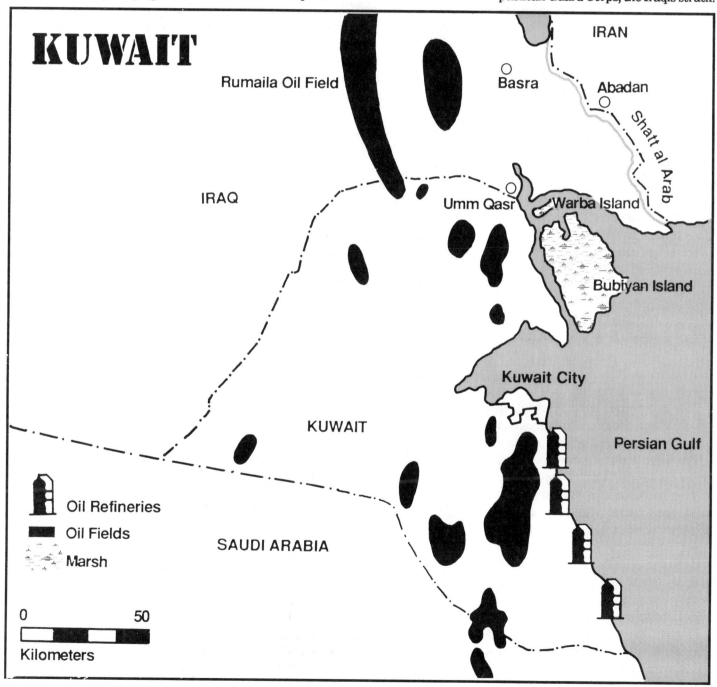

KUWAIT

Rumaila Oil Field

IRAN

Basra

Abadan

Shatt al Arab

IRAQ

Umm Qasr

Warba Island

Bubiyan Island

KUWAIT

Kuwait City

Persian Gulf

Oil Refineries

Oil Fields

Marsh

SAUDI ARABIA

0   50

Kilometers

MODERN MILITARY
JARGON & SYMBOLS

The military has a language and a symbology all its own. This section will do its best to explain some of the more common words and phrases used, and to make them more intelligible to the average person.

UNIT SIZES

Armies are constructed of a hierarchy of units. Many small units are organized into larger and larger units.

Squad: A unit consisting of six to 12 soldiers, usually led by a sergeant. Squads are the basic building block of a unit, and in most armies the squad is the smallest unit.

Section: A section is a unit intermediate in size between a squad and a platoon. A section contains 15-30 soldiers, and is usually led by a senior sergeant. The British Army uses the term *section* for squad.

Platoon: A platoon consists of three to four sections or squads (40-50 soldiers), plus a platoon leader (usually a lieutenant) and an assistant platoon leader (a senior sergeant).

Company: A company consists of three to five platoons, plus a headquarters, and is usually commanded by a captain.

Troop: A troop is a company-sized unit of cavalry. In British usage, a troop is a platoon-sized armored or mechanized cavalry unit. When British and US units operate together, this can be a source of confusion. (See also *Squadron*.)

Battery: A battery is a group of artillery pieces of some kind, and is usually company-sized in terms of the number of personnel involved.

Flight: The smallest air force unit. Typically, a flight consists of four aircraft and is commanded by a major.

Battalion: A battalion consists of three to five companies plus a headquarters company. It is usually commanded by a lieutenant colonel.

Squadron: In the US Army a squadron is a battalion-sized unit of cavalry. In the British Army it is a company-sized unit of tanks or armored cars.

In air forces, a squadron has 12-24 aircraft, all of the same type and intended to conduct the same mission. An air force squadron is commanded by a lieutenant colonel.

Regiment: A regiment consists of a number of battalions, usually three to five, plus a headquarters unit. It is usually commanded by a colonel. In many armies (including those of Britain and France) a *regiment* means a battalion.

Group: In armies, a group generally has two or more battalions, while in air forces it has two or more squadrons. Groups are typically commanded by a colonel.

Brigade: A brigade consists of a number of battalions, usually three to six. It is usually commanded by a colonel or a brigadier general (one star).

Wing: In the US Air Force, a wing has three flying squadrons. In the USMC it has several groups of squadrons. Wings are commanded by colonels or brigadier generals (one star).

Division: A division consists of a number of brigades or regiments (usually three), plus smaller supporting units (battalions or companies). It is usually commanded by a major general (two stars). The division is the largest unit for which a formal table of organization exists.

Air Division: A headquarters for up to three wings. Wings sometimes report directly to a numbered air force. Commanded by major generals (two stars).

Corps: A corps contains several divisions, the exact number depending upon its intended mission, plus smaller supporting units. A corps is usually commanded by a lieutenant general (three stars).

Numbered Air Force: Typically the headquarters for all air units in a theater of operations or major sub-theater. Commanded by a lieutenant general (three stars).

Army: An army consists of several corps, plus supporting units. It is usually commanded by a general (four stars).

UNIT SYMBOLS

The organizational diagrams in this book make use of a standard set of military symbols. The system consists of a rectangular box symbol identifying the troop type, a unit size indicator atop it, and various numbers and letters giving more information about the unit. Nationality is to the left of the rectangle, and the unit's identifying number or other data is to the right.

In the sample, the rectangle with the oval in it represents an armored unit. The "XX" atop it indicates that it is a division. The "US" to the left of the rectangle gives nationality and the "3" to the right indicates that the unit is the US 3rd Armored Division. Multiple units are represented, as shown by the example, by "stacking" several rectangles (the symbol represents three artillery battalions).

Sometimes unit type symbols are combined: Note, for example that the mechanized infantry symbol combines the infantry and armor symbols.

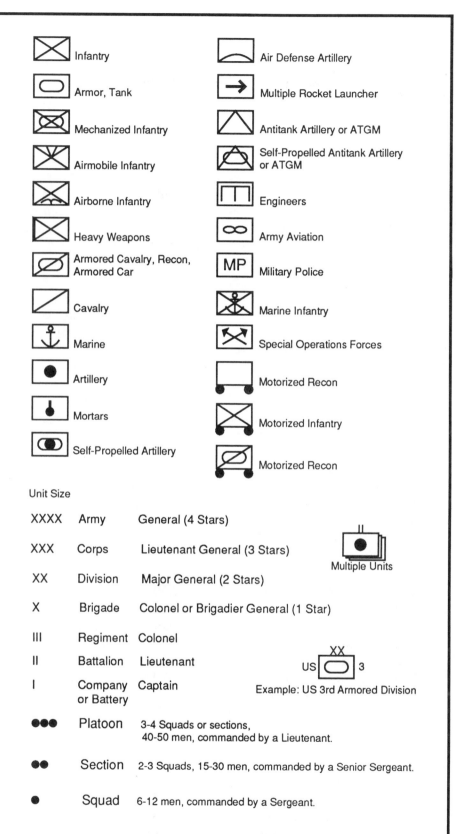

Symbol	Name		Symbol	Name
	Infantry			Air Defense Artillery
	Armor, Tank			Multiple Rocket Launcher
	Mechanized Infantry			Antitank Artillery or ATGM
	Airmobile Infantry			Self-Propelled Antitank Artillery or ATGM
	Airborne Infantry			Engineers
	Heavy Weapons			Army Aviation
	Armored Cavalry, Recon, Armored Car			Military Police
	Cavalry			Marine Infantry
	Marine			Special Operations Forces
	Artillery			Motorized Recon
	Mortars			Motorized Infantry
	Self-Propelled Artillery			Motorized Recon

Unit Size

XXXX	Army	General (4 Stars)
XXX	Corps	Lieutenant General (3 Stars)
XX	Division	Major General (2 Stars)
X	Brigade	Colonel or Brigadier General (1 Star)
III	Regiment	Colonel
II	Battalion	Lieutenant
I	Company or Battery	Captain
●●●	Platoon	3-4 Squads or sections, 40-50 men, commanded by a Lieutenant.
●●	Section	2-3 Squads, 15-30 men, commanded by a Senior Sergeant.
●	Squad	6-12 men, commanded by a Sergeant.

Multiple Units

Example: US 3rd Armored Division

UNIT SYMBOLS
Based on NATO Standards

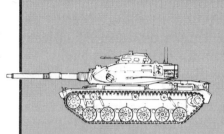

GULF WAR
FACT BOOK
Jargon and Symbols

WHAT IS A TANK?

One of the most commonly made errors in military reporting is confusion of tank with armored vehicle. A tank is a tracked, heavily armored vehicle whose principal purpose is to carry a heavy direct-fire cannon. Often reporters mistake anything with a turret for a tank. The Soviet-built BMP is often called a tank, as is the US Bradley IFV. Although they are tracked vehicles and have turrets, they fail to qualify as tanks on three grounds. First, they are lightly armored. Second, they carry a comparatively small gun. Third, their main purpose is not to carry the gun system, but rather to transport infantry. The M109 self-propelled howitzer is also sometimes mistaken for a tank, but it doesn't qualify because it is lightly armored and its gun is for indirect fire, not direct fire.

MILITARY TERMS

The military needs a special vocabulary because it deals with special equipment and activities. These are some of the words they use.

AFV. *Armored Fighting Vehicle.* A vehicle intended to engage in combat, which means it is armored and armed. AFV covers several types of vehicles, including tanks, APCs, CFVs, and IFVs.

AOR. *Area of Responsibility.* The portion of a combat zone for which a commander is responsible.

APC. *Armored Personnel Carrier.* An armored personnel carrier is an AFV whose primary mission is to transport infantry around the battlefield. It is usually lightly armored (to protect the passengers from small arms fire and shell fragments).

ARM. *Antiradiation Missile.* ARMs are missiles equipped to seek out and home in on radar emissions. They are primarily used by airplanes to attack enemy antiaircraft radars.

Armored. This means that the vehicle is equipped with protection for its passengers and crew. Heavily armored means that a vehicle is capable of resisting main gun hits. Lightly armored means that a vehicle is capable of resisting hits from small arms fire and shell fragments.

ATGM. *Antitank Guided Missile.* A guided missile is a weapon that uses the thrust of a rocket motor to propel it to the target (and does so constantly throughout its flight), and is capable of making course corrections that guide it toward a target, even if that target is moving.

ATGW. *Antitank Guided Weapon.* Technically any guided warhead intended to defeat armored vehicles, including CLGP (see below). In practice, it is usually synonymous with ATGM. ATGMs and ATGWs are usually of two types: beam riders, which follow a beam of laser or infrared radiation to their target (a human has to constantly keep the beam on the target in order for the missile to guide on it), and wire-guided, which follow guidance instructions from a complex electronic sight (which also has to be kept pointed at the target).

AWACS. *Airborne Warning and Control System.* An aircraft-mounted radar system used to detect enemy aircraft and direct defenses to intercept them.

BDA. *Battle (or Bomb) Damage Assessment.* The reconnaissance, analysis, and judgment of the effects of attacks.

Blister Agent. This is a form of chemical weapon that attacks the skin of its victims, causing chemical burns. Gas masks and protective clothing will work against this weapon.

Blood Agent. This is a form of chemical weapon that must be inhaled to kill. Masks provide adequate protection against this type of weapon.

CBR. *Chemical, Biological, Radiological.* The military speciality concerned with these three types of warfare. At times, the speciality has been called ABC (atomic, biological, chemical) and NBC (nuclear, biological, chemical).

CEP. *Circular Error Probability.* A measure of the accuracy of missiles, artillery rounds, or bombs. The CEP is the radius of a circle sized so that half the rounds fired from a weapon will fall inside it. If the CEP of a weapon is 100 feet, each attack by the weapon has a 50% chance of hitting within 100 feet of where it was aimed.

CFV. *Cavalry Fighting Vehicle.* A type of AFV intended for scouting or recon purposes. These vehicles are sometimes called armored cars, and are lightly armored, although they may be heavily armed.

Chobham. A type of composite armor developed by the British, and incorporated into the design of the M1 Abrams tank. A diagram of Chobham armor is shown in the section discussing the M1 tank.

CLGP. *Cannon-Launched Guided Projectile.* This is a ballistic weapon, which means that it does not have thrust propelling it throughout its flight path, but it does have fins and a complex electronic guidance system enabling it to be guided to its target.

Collateral Damage. Any unintentional damage resulting from an attack. Often considered to be a code phase for civilian casualties, collateral damage actually has a much broader meaning. If an ammo truck is attacked and the secondary explosions from its ammunition destroy a nearby combat vehicle, that is collateral damage.

Direct Fire. Weapons with direct fire shoot at targets the firer can see (although the round may not follow a straight line to get there). Some weapons may be used in both direct and indirect fire (see *Indirect Fire*).

EW. *Electronic Warfare.* The use of radar and electronics to detect, mislead, or counter enemy activity.

FASCAM. *Field Artillery Scatterable Minefield.* This is an artillery round containing a number of antitank or antipersonnel mines. It is a means of laying a minefield quickly and with minimal risk.

FLIR. *Forward-Looking Infrared.* The night vision device used on Allied aircraft that provides detailed images based on the heat radiated by an object. Similar in principle to thermal vision devices.

Force Package. A temporary grouping of several aircraft, sometimes of different types, to perform a specific mission. Also called a force packet.

HEAT. *High Explosive Antitank.* A type of warhead that relies on a high-velocity stream of molten metal to punch through armor. This high-speed stream of metal is generated by the burning of a carefully shaped explosive charge.

Heavy Forces. Heavy forces are units containing tanks or combined arms teams of tanks, mechanized infantry, and self-propelled artillery. Heavy forces are capable of delivering devastating firepower, but tend to be very expensive in fuel and ammunition. They often take (and cause) heavy casualties.

ICM. *Improved Conventional Munitions.* A form of artillery projectile containing a number of smaller grenades. At a fixed distance above the ground, the ICM shell casing fractures and the smaller grenades (sometimes called *bomblets*) are scattered over a wide area, exploding on contact with the ground, or at a preset height of one to three meters.

IFV. *Infantry Fighting Vehicle.* An AFV intended to transport infantry on the battlefield and provide combat support with its own armor-defeating weapons as well. The US M2 Bradley and the Soviet-designed BMP are IFVs.

Indirect Fire. Indirect fire is directed against targets which the firer cannot see, usually from information received from forward observers, observation aircraft, or recon vehicles. All long-range artillery fire is indirect fire.

MBT. *Main Battle Tank.* A heavily armored AFV carrying a large-caliber main weapon, capable of participating in the most intense fighting. The US MBT is the Abrams.

Mechanized. Infantry which ride in APCs or IFVs. Such infantry can move faster, carry more and heavier weapons, and strike harder than nonmechanized infantry.

MLRS. *Multiple-Launch Rocket System.* A weapon for launching "volleys" of several rockets at once or in rapid succession. Most MLRSs are mounted on vehicles, and are self-propelled.

MOS. *Military Occupational Specialty.* The specific training and experience background for a soldier. The MOS for many soldiers is simply infantryman or tank crew. For others, it is vehicle mechanic, clerk, or radar technician. There are thousands of MOS designations.

Motorized. Infantry which ride in trucks or other unarmored vehicles. The chief advantage of such infantry is speed.

MRL. *Multiple-Rocket Launcher.* This can be another name for an MLRS, but some MRLs are towed rather than self-propelled.

Nerve Agent. A form of chemical weapon that attacks the nervous system and can be absorbed through the skin. This is the most deadly form of chemical weapon, as a single drop on exposed skin can be fatal within minutes. Masks and full suits are required for protection.

Platform. The navy term for any of its vessels. A ship or a submarine is a platform (for weapons).

Republican Guards. Elite troops of the Iraqi regime. They are the most reliable and best-equipped forces available.

RPV. *Remotely Piloted Vehicle.* A flying observation drone carrying a television camera used to observe artillery fire. Used both by land forces and by naval gunfire vessels, including the two US battleships in the war.

SAM. *Surface-to-Air Missile.* A missile intended to be fired at aircraft from the ground, usually incorporating some form of homing device enabling it to guide itself to its target.

SAS. *Special Air Service.* The British equivalent of special forces.

Special Forces. In Western usage, commando-style elite light troops designed for clandestine and unconventional missions. In the Iraqi Army they are heavily armed assault troops.

Sortie. One flight by one aircraft.

Sortie Rate. The number of flights an aircraft makes in a day, or the average number of sorties per plane in a force.

SSM. *Surface-to-Surface Missile.* A missile intended to be fired from the ground at another target on the ground. These include both guided and unguided missiles.

Task Force. In army terms, a task force is a combined arms force of approximately battalion strength. In naval terms, a task force is a temporary grouping of various vessels structured to accomplish a specific mission.

Theater. A geographical area within which a war or a campaign in a war is fought. In a small war, "the theater" may refer to the entire area of hostilities. In a major war, there may be several geographically distinct theaters.

Thermal Sights. Thermal sights make use of the heat generated by a target to detect it, even in total darkness.

Zulu. The designation for the standard Greenwich Mean Time (GMT) zone. The 24 time zones around the world are designated with alphabetic letters. In global military operations, GMT or Zulu time is used.

RIVAL BATTLE DOCTRINES
AIRLAND BATTLE

Doctrine is one of those terms that is more used than understood. By doctrine, we mean a set of guiding principles and specific procedures by which an army fights a war. Strategy has guiding principles of its own, but doctrine usually refers to the way in which an army conducts operations and tactical actions. So an army can have both tactical and operational doctrines.

Which brings us to some more interesting military jargon: strategy, operations, and tactics—also terms that are more used than understood. What is the difference?

Strategy is the establishment of political goals of a country engaged in a dispute. If military forces are involved, strategy defines the key military objectives which must be achieved to attain those political goals.

Operations are the allocation of specific forces to specific military objectives. Operational planning provides a blueprint for the employment of those forces.

Tactics are the means by which each of those specific forces achieves its specific objective within the overall operational plan.

For example, the *strategy* of the Gulf War was to force Iraq to withdraw from Kuwait and to eliminate its offensive war-making potential. The *operational plan* adopted was a pinning attack in the east and a wide envelopment from the west, thus isolating and eventually destroying the Iraqi forces in the Kuwaiti Theater of Operations. The *tactics* used involved artillery preparation, air assaults, fast-moving tank columns, and deliberate breaching operations against the fortified Saddam Line.

THE GENESIS OF AIRLAND BATTLE

Historically, the United States has relied on a tactical doctrine of position and firepower. That is, Army and Marine units are taught to make maximum use of covering terrain and to bring maximum firepower to bear to destroy an enemy force. Although generals preached mobility in a general sense, the actual training emphasized fire and close maneuver.

As the US Army began taking the Soviet conventional ground threat in Europe seriously in the 1970s, officers began taking a closer look at how the Red Army fought. What they found was encouraging at first glance. Tactics were stereotyped: units used rehearsed responses to stereotyped battle situations, and were very predictable at the lower levels. These clumsy battlefield tactics would go a long way to offset superior numbers, just as they had for the Germans in World War II. The triumph of a "Western-style" Israeli Army over the "Soviet-style" Arab armies in several wars further supported this view.

Upon closer examination, there were nagging inconsistencies. The more historical material that was unearthed on the Red Army in World War II, the thinner its numeric advantage began to appear, and the better its operational planning and execution looked. While Soviet tactical doctrine was simple and rigid, Soviet operational doctrine was rich and frighteningly well thought-out.

This operational level was an area to which the United States had never devoted as much attention as it deserved. Here fundamental differences divided armies into two broad categories: those devoted to maneuver at the operational level and those devoted to position and firepower. In the latter category could be placed the British, US, and Arab armies, while in the former category were found the Germans, Soviets, and Israelis. Gradually, the lessons of the Arab-Israeli wars became less convincing vindications of our style of warfare.

As the US military establishment developed a growing understanding of, and appreciation for, what the Soviets call "operational art," there developed tremendous pressure for a fundamental change in US doctrine. The result was a major doctrinal initiative from the US Training and Doctrine Command (TRADOC), under the direction of General Donn A. Starry. It was called AirLand Battle.

IMPORTANT FEATURES

AirLand Battle contains many features of the mobile doctrines used by the Red Army, the Germans, and the Israelis, but also includes numerous unique elements. Several important features may help to understand it, and mobile warfare in general.

Attack: You cannot win a battle, or war, without attacking. Failure to attack allows the enemy to decide when and where the battle will be fought. A defensive success, if not followed up by an attack, just lets the enemy withdraw and try again later. If he gets to keep trying, eventually he will succeed.

Maneuver: Positional armies move so that they can be in a better position to fight, and view fire as the ultimate means by which an opponent is destroyed. Mobile armies fight so that they can break out and maneuver, and view the movement of masses of troops behind the enemy front as a means, *in and of itself,* of disrupting the enemy force. For example, the movement of VII Corps and XVIII Airborne Corps deep into the Iraqi rear caused tremendous disruption to the enemy forces, apart from the physical damage caused by their advance.

Objective: Identify the single most important objective, the one which will guarantee a successful conclusion of the battle, and concentrate everything on it. This means concentration in time as well as space; all critical blows should be delivered as close to simultaneously as possible, even if they are in different geographic areas. It also means concentration of the commander's and staff's mental energies. In the gulf, the objective was the Republican Guard; it might as well have had a bull's-eye painted on it.

Activity: One of the catch phrases of AirLand Battle is "getting inside the enemy's decision cycle." What does that mean?

An event takes place, a commander gets the report of the event, he makes a decision for his troops, communicates it to the troops, and then they act. This is a complete decision cycle. If, in the meantime, the enemy has taken a different action, then by the time the commander's order gets to his troops, it is no longer relevant to the changing situation. That is what is meant by getting inside his decision cycle. The way a force does that is by continuous, purposeful activity.

Once an operation is launched, it should continue nonstop and full speed until it is either called off completely of it achieves its goal.

IRAQI DOCTRINE

Did the Iraqis use Soviet doctrine? Perhaps tactical doctrine, but clearly not operational doctrine. The performance of the Iraqi Army during the eight years of the Iran-Iraq War showed it to be a force solidly committed to positional warfare. It had no talent for, or even concept of, operational maneuver. The tempo of combat it was used to was one or two orders of magnitude less than

that which 3rd Army imposed on it. Even had their command control structure been intact, the lightning speed and concentrated violence of 3rd Army's attack would have caused total sensory overload and a command control system collapse.

HOW WOULD IVAN DO IT?

The classic Soviet response to the situation in the KTO, as dictated by the Soviet conception of mobile warfare, would probably read as follows:

The front will engage the main fortified position of the enemy with the combined arms armies of the front, using their infantry and artillery assets to engage and pin the enemy in place.

Front will form an operational maneuver group (OMG) by heavily reinforcing a division of the front with extra armor and air assault assets. The OMG will move through the front on a lightly defended sector, avoiding all contact with the enemy if possible, and race deep into his rear area to sow confusion and disrupt his command centers, artillery positions, and reserves.

Once the enemy infantry is pinned and enemy reserves committed, the front's tank army will strike at the point in the line offering the greatest prospect of a quick breakthrough, preferably on a flank. It will follow the advance of the front OMG and deliver the decisive blow against the enemy's center of gravity from the flank or rear.

The front's air assault brigade, plus that of the tank army, will penetrate the enemy front ahead of the tank army and seize choke points in his rear, cutting of his avenues of escape.

Light forces and recon units, and frontal aviation assets, will screen the flanks of the breakthrough and prevent the intervention of enemy against the tank army breakthrough.

If VII Corps is considered the tank army, French 6th Light Armored the screening force, 101st Air Assault the combined air assault assets, 24th Mech the OMG, and the marines and Joint Forces Command troops the combined arms armies, the above is broadly similar to Central Command's plan of attack. There are still important differences, though, which illustrate the uniquely American approach brought to AirLand Battle.

HITTING THE MARK
DIRECT FIRE GUNNERY

As tanks are the most deadly close combat system on the modern battlefield, armies spend a good deal of effort trying to knock out those of the enemy. There are three main weapon systems used to deal with tanks once they are in close combat: high velocity guns (usually mounted on friendly tanks), guided antitank missiles, and unguided infantry-carried antitank rockets. The first step in knocking out a tank with any of these is actually hitting it.

TANK GUNS

Engaging an enemy tank with your own tank gun is complicated by a number of variables, and the gunner must generate a solution to each of these variables in order to achieve a hit.

The Old Fashioned Way: On tanks equipped with optic sights, a gunner engages enemy tanks the same way they did in World War II. To ensure a hit, the gunner has to follow several steps. The illustration to the right shows a typical sight picture for a tank with an optical range finder.

1. Range: The farther away the target, the more the gun has to be elevated to hit it. But the gunner has to know exactly, or nearly so, how far away it is to determine how much to elevate his gun.

The bottom right quarter of the sight shows a ranging reticle graduated in 200 meter increments, from 1000 to 3000 meters. The gunner traverses and elevates the gun until that target tank is in the reticle. He then lines it up so that the bottom of the tank is flush with the bottom line and the top touches one of the range lines. This tells him the range within 200 meters, assuming the target is 2.7 meters tall (the typical height of a Western tank). If it is shorter (which the M1A1 is) or partially hidden, or falls somewhere between the lines, the gunner makes a guess.

2. Ammunition: Different types of ammunition fired from the same gun have different ballistic characteristics. Therefore the correct range elevation for APFSDS will cause HEAT rounds, which have uniformly lower velocities, to fall considerably short of the target. The gunner adjusts the range line (which runs all the way across the sight from left to right) to the correct range on the scale corresponding to the ammunition type being fired. Where that line now intersects the centerline of the sight (indicated by the large arrow at the bottom) is the gunner's aiming point. He now traverses the turret and elevates or depresses the gun until that target is centered at the aiming point.

3. Lead: If the tank is moving, the gunner has to lead it. He estimates the speed and traverses the gun right or left to compensate for its movement.

4. Cant: If the gunner knows the

Reticle of the Soviet TSh2B-41u gunner's telescope. This is the scope picture as seen by the gunner of a T-55 or T-62 tank.

range to the target, he simply elevates the gun the correct amount and fires. However, if the tank is canted (tilted to one side), elevating the gun will not just move it up; it will move it up and slightly to one side, causing the round to miss. If the tank is canted (and it's a lucky tank crew that can always find perfectly level ground) the gunner must somehow compensate for this by aiming slightly higher and to the opposite direction from the cant. He makes a guess.

5. Crosswind: Crosswinds are not a great problem when firing at close range, but at progressively longer ranges they become more and more important. Also, modern high-velocity tank rounds are particularly susceptible to crosswinds because they are fin-stabilized.

A crosswind pushes on all parts of a rifled round the with equal force.

As a result, it will push it to the side a little, but it won't alter its course. With a finned round, however, the wind affects the tail of the round much more than the front, and so actually twists the round. Instead of blowing it downwind, it will tend to turn it upwind.

Unless the gunner can accurately gauge the effects of crosswinds, it is very difficult to hit a target at long range, and it is almost impossible to know the wind speed and direction while buttoned up in a tank.

6. Barrel Droop: A tank's gunsights assume that the barrel is straight, or at least droops at a uniform rate. In combat, however, repeated firings of the gun will cause it to heat up, and as it does so the barrel begins to droop. This is also a problem in hot climates, as the sun makes the top of the gun barrel much hotter than the shaded bottom, thus distorting it and causing it to droop. This changes the ballistics of the gun, enough so that the gunner must compensate for it or the rounds will begin to fall short. If the round falls short, the gunner just elevates a little and tries again.

7. Barrel Wear: As a gun is fired, the barrel wears out, and the older it is, the more worn it becomes. This also affects the ballistics of the rounds fired from the tank, and the same procedure used for barrel droop is followed.

The Modern Solution: A gunner in a tank equipped with a modern laser range finder and a ballistic computer has a much easier job. The gunner elects an ammunition type by punching a single button on his ballistic computer and then centers the gun sight on the target. He triggers the laser range finder which measures the range to the target accurately to within a few meters. The ballistic computer then calculates the correct elevation for

the ammunition being used, measures the cant angle, barrel droop, barrel wear, and wind speed (using a wind sensor on the turret roof) and automatically adjusts the traverse and elevation of the gun. The gun sight remains stationary on the target. Once the gun is correctly laid, the gunner fires and, more often than not, hits the target.

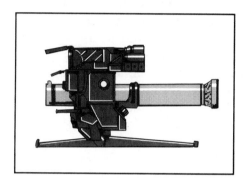

ANTITANK GUIDED MISSILES

It takes a very heavy vehicle, capable of absorbing tremendous recoil energy, to mount a large caliber, high-velocity gun. For lighter vehicles, the weapon of choice is the antitank missile.

A missile has no recoil, since its own motor accelerates it out of the firing tube (or off a rail) and flies it downrange to the target. The gunner steers the missile to the target, and so it is capable of great accuracy at long ranges.

Most missiles are wire-guided. That means that the missile is connected to the launcher by a thin wire that unwinds behind the missile as it flies. A few missiles are beam riders, meaning they receive guidance commands from the launcher by radio, laser, or infrared beams. The Hellfire missile fired from the US Apache attack helicopter homes in on the reflection of a laser designator. The target can be designated by either the firing helicopter or an observation helicopter.

ANTITANK ROCKET LAUNCHERS

Most missiles are too heavy for an infantryman to carry. For close-in defense against enemy armor, the infantryman carries an antitank rocket launcher (ATRL). This fires an unguided rocket, so the infantryman must aim at the enemy tank and faces many of the same problems as does a tank gunner, but with none of the high-tech aids. Like missiles, ATRLs rely on a low-velocity round with a HEAT warhead

There are two general types of ATRLs: disposable and reloadable. Reloadable launchers, such as the RPG-7 and Carl Gustav, tend to be heavier, but the individual rounds are lighter. Also, reloadable launchers tend to be more accurate. Disposable launchers, such as LAW-80 and AT-4, are more suitable for issuing to a large number of troops. Both types of weapons have short ranges, but are murderous in close terrain, such as in cities and fortified areas.

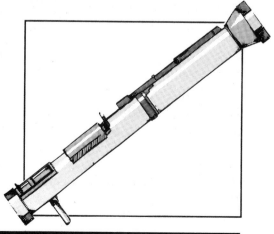

PUNCHING ARMOR
PIERCING THE SHELL

Tanks and other armored vehicles rely on armor for protection from enemy weapons. Most armored personnel carriers (APCs) have very light armor, intended only to keep out small arms fire and enemy artillery fragments. Tanks, however, have considerably thicker armor intended to defeat some or all of the enemy's anti-tank weapons.

Subsequent pages list the armor protection of the main tanks and other armored vehicles which served during the war. In all cases, the value shown is the estimated average protection throughout the frontal arc of the vehicle (which is where most enemy fire comes from). Because heavy armor on all faces would be prohibitively heavy, tanks always have less protection on their sides and rear. Weapons unable to penetrate the front armor of the tank can still be effective if they are positioned for flank or rear shots, but this is difficult and hazardous.

All armor is listed in its equivalent to hardened armor plate. The term "equivalent" is important here, because most tanks have armor considerably thinner than the values shown. However, tank armor is usually angled against attack from the most likely direction. Extreme angles increase the chance that an enemy round will glance off, but any angling of the armor increases the effective thickness of armor that a round may penetrate.

As a rough rule of thumb, armor angled at 30° from vertical is about 50% more effective than its nominal thickness while armor angled at 60° from vertical is about twice as effective.

Note that some tanks have two different armor thicknesses shown, one for conventional rounds and a second (greater) one for HEAT rounds. These are tanks with either Chobham or reactive armor.

HOW ANTITANK ROUNDS WORK

There is a wide variety of antitank rounds, but two types predominate: armor-piercing fin-stabilized discarding sabot (APFSDS) and high explosive antitank (HEAT).

APFSDS is fired from both rifled and smoothbore guns. A finned, dart-shaped penetrator is encased in a two- or three-piece sabot (*SAY-bow*) of a lightweight material, such as aluminum. The lightness of the round means that the powder charge accelerates it to extremely high velocities. Upon leaving the gun tube the sabot falls away, while the penetrator hurtles downrange and pierces the target's armor.

HEAT rounds can be fired from guns, but may also be the warheads of light rockets or wire-guided missiles. This is so because the round does not rely on the velocity of the projectile to generate energy. Instead, the round detonates when it hits the target.

HEAT has a *shaped charge* warhead that directs the explosion for-

---

CHOBHAM ARMOR

Chobham armor was developed at the Chobham arsenal in the United Kingdom, hence its name. It is a unique blend of ceramic blocks in a resin matrix sandwiched between sheets of conventional armor plate. This armor is very effective against conventional tank guns, but is extraordinarily so against HEAT rounds, which arm most infantry-carried antitank rockets and antitank guided missiles. The armor used on US tanks is slightly different than true British Chobham armor, and is slightly more effective against HEAT rounds, but is constructed along identical principles.

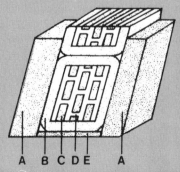

A. Conventional steel outer and inner armor plates. B. Aluminum or plastic inner casing. C. Ceramic blocks. D. Epoxy or other special glue matrix. E. Additional armor sheet holds armor blocks in place. In some versions the blocks are held in place by bolts.

A B C D E   A

ward. A molten stream of metal blasts forward and this metal stream acts just like the solid penetrator of the APFSDS round.

For a very long time it was thought that HEAT rounds actually burned their way through armor, but engineers have now shown that the fluid dynamics equations describing penetration by APFSDS rounds also describe the penetration by the metallic jet of a HEAT round.

The advantage of HEAT is that it does not require a high projectile velocity to work, so it doesn't need a gun system to generate that velocity. Infantrymen cannot carry around a tank gun, but they can carry around a low-velocity rocket launcher with a HEAT warhead. Similarly, wire-guided missiles give infantry and light vehicles a potent long-range antitank capability.

The disadvantage of HEAT is that the penetrator jet is easily disrupted, degrading the ability of the round to penetrate and destroy. The two main means of disrupting the jet are Chobham armor and reactive armor.

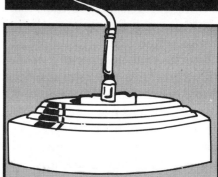

ANTITANK MINES

Although most antitank weapons attempt to defeat a tank's armor, all that is really necessary is to immobilize it. Mines are excellent for that purpose, and Iraq used large numbers of them in the so-called "Saddam Line."

All a mine is composed of is an explosive charge and a detonator. This can be a command detonator, magnetic detonator, or any of a variety of exotic types, but the most common is a simple pressure detonator. When the tank drives over the mine, it blows up and breaks its tracks (at least).

Although Coalition engineers did a good job dealing with Iraqi mines, antitank mines still disabled a number of Egyptian tanks as they broke into the fortification line. As many or more Coalition tanks were lost to mines as to enemy tank gun fire.

REACTIVE ARMOR

Reactive armor is extremely simple in principle. It consists of a number of explosive blocks fastened to the outside of an armored vehicle which explode when hit by an enemy high-energy round. (They are usually designed so that machinegun fire will not detonate them, at least in theory.) While reactive armor has little effect on conventional armor-piercing rounds, it is very effective against HEAT rounds, as it degrades their penetration by disrupting their penetrator jets.

While the exact physics of reactive armor are still being studied, the closest explanation of the mechanics to date is that the explosion of the block blows the block's cover plate up and away at an angle while the penetrator jet is still passing through it, thus removing considerable mass from the penetrator stream itself.

The first army to employ reactive armor was the Israeli Defense Force in Lebanon. It was used because tanks were forced to more into built up urban areas where enemy infantry antitank teams could easily approach with handheld rocket launchers. The Soviet army followed suit soon after and launched a major effort to incorporate reactive armor arrays on its tank forces in Europe as a counter to NATO's superiority in antitank missiles. Soviet reactive armor, which probably has fairly typical performance, is believed to add about 250mm worth of protection to the tank against HEAT-type warheads.

Fortunately, no reactive armor blocks are believed to have reached Iraq prior to the arms embargo, and no Iraqi tanks have been observed with either reactive armor itself or the mounting brackets needed for its use.

The only tanks in the Persian Gulf theater using reactive armor are the M60 tanks of the US Marine Corps, often shown in television news reports with their large, easily recognizable sheets of reactive armor blocks on the turret and chassis front.

ENGINEER OPERATIONS
BREACHING BARRIERS

Engineers are specialists at overcoming obstacles. Sometimes those obstacles are natural, sometimes they are man-made. Sometimes the obstacle is the absence of a needed structure, such as a road or bridge. At other times it is the presence of a barrier, such as a crater, minefield, or ditch. In all of these case, engineers are tasked with getting the troops across the obstacle and moving again.

CONSTRUCTION TASKS

The Arabian peninsula is very thinly inhabited, with the result that there is a very sparse infrastructure of roads and buildings available. Although the years leading up to the Gulf War had seen a large number of air bases built, there was still a need for runways and shelters. Troops lacked barracks, and while they could live under canvas for a while, in the long run that could be damaging to health and morale.

The major engineering tasks confronted in the KTO were infrastructure construction tasks linked to the above shortages. Roads, airfields, and barracks were all needed, and in large numbers. Maintenance of existing roads was important as well; the few roads available coupled with the large supply and troop movement demands, meant that the roads were subjected to nearly constant heavy traffic.

BREACHING OPERATIONS

As important as road building was to the campaign, an interest in the combat support functions of engineers is natural. Combat engineers, in addition to being equipped for construction tasks, have a variety of vehicles and devices suited for breaching and clearing obstacles. The most obvious one is the bulldozer. Dozers were used extensively to open breaches in the sand berms along the border. Sometimes these were specially outfitted dozer tanks, but more often they were standard unarmored earthmovers.

Minefields were a special concern to the marines and Joint Forces Command troops tasked with breaching the Saddam Line. A variety of means were used to clear paths through minefields. One of the more common was the mine plow fitted to the front of a standard tank. These are the cultivator-like devices seen in a number of videotape shots of tanks shortly before the attack. When lowered, these cut into the ground. The blades slide under mines, lift them up, and push them to the sides. If the mine detonates, it does so away from the tank itself.

A second important device is the explosive line charge. This is a rocket attached to a flexible hose filled with explosives. The rocket is fired and flies over the minefield, dragging the hose behind it. When the hose is in position on top of the field, engineers fire it and the concussion detonates any mines directly under it. This clears a path wide enough for troops and tanks to go through.

Fuel air explosives (FAE) were also used to clear gaps through minefields. These air-dropped weapons discharge a large volume of fuel in the air over a target. Once it is dispersed into an aerosol, a delayed charge detonator (suspended from a parachute) goes off and causes a tremendous explosion. The overpressure on the ground detonates mines over a large area.

Specialized bridging vehicles (modified tanks carrying "scissors" bridges) are used to cross antitank ditches and narrow ravines. Special combat engineer vehicles are often equipped with large-bore, short-range demolition guns and heavy cranes. Any obstacle the crane can't lift out of the way, the demolition gun blows out of the way.

M728 CEV

THE SADDAM LINE

Convinced that a Coalition attack would come across the Kuwaiti border from the south, the Iraqis constructed an elaborate fortification system later dubbed the Saddam Line. Although the fortifications were not always constructed with the care implied by the neat diagrams seen in army manuals and newspapers (and here, for that matter), there were still formidable barriers.

The basis of the fortifications was a series of triangular battalion forts (see sidebar) that housed the main strength of the front-line infantry divisions. A division might deploy to a depth of 10 kilometers, but the rear areas were mostly occupied by artillery and support troops. The combat troops tended to be deployed in a solid crust, with depth in the position being achieved by layering divisions one behind another.

In front of the chain of battalion

forts were the obstacles themselves. These consisted of several layers of antitank ditches, oil ditches, wire entanglements, and minefields. Over a half million mines may have been emplaced along the Kuwaiti border. Where time or labor assets did not allow digging of a proper antitank ditch, a more shallow ditch was used which was filled with oil. The intent was to ignite these with thermite or phosphorus charges when the attack drew near. Marine Harriers dropped napalm along these ditches for several days before the attack to burn off the oil, and few if any of these ditches were successfully ignited during the actual attack.

So extensive were the obstacle barriers that there were insufficient troops available to maintain them. When sand drifts over minefields, or mudslides cover them, the mines are either detonated or rendered harmless by the extra covering. Antitank ditches silt in. Oil ditches empty as the oil soaks into the ground. All of these natural events served to degrade the effectiveness of the fortifications. Nevertheless, they remained a formidable barrier.

In the final analysis, fortifications are only as good as the troops in them. By the time the ground attack was launched, most of the Iraqi garrisons were thoroughly cowed. Had they fought harder, the outcome would have been the same, but the Coalition would have had to pay a much higher price in blood to achieve it.

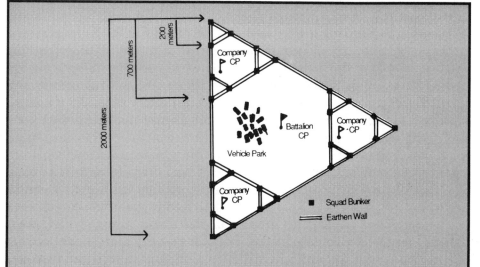

THE TRIANGULAR BATTALION FORT

Iraqi infantry brigades usually entrenched on an eight-kilometer front, with the front line consisting of three triangular battalion forts at five-kilometer intervals. Each fort was an equilateral triangle about two kilometers across, with each side formed by a bulldozed wall of packed dirt or sand two-to-four meters in height. All of the battalion's vehicles were parked in the middle of the fort.

The actual fighting positions were on the points of the fort, with one company position at each corner. Each of the company positions consisted of three platoon forts in a triangular layout, and each platoon complex consisted of three squad positions, also in a triangular layout. The company forts were about 700 meters across, the platoon forts about 200 meters. Each squad fighting position was designed for all-around fire, and was usually built from packed earth reinforced by steel mesh and/or concrete. Each sub-unit placed its command post and heavy weapons in the center of the fighting position. Each fort was surrounded by barbed wire and minefields, when sufficient engineering supplies were available.

The Iraqi forts in Kuwait were fronted by three belts of mines, each separated by an antitank ditch. Barrels of gasoline were placed in many of the ditches with remote explosive charges that could be command-detonated from the Iraqi positions.

GUNS AND ROTORS
FIRE SUPPORT

The traditional means of delivering fire support to forward units has been by artillery fire, and that is still the most important. Traditional tube artillery is now supplemented by sophisticated multiple-rocket launchers, helicopter gunships, and tactical ground-attack aircraft. All of these means of ground support have something in common, however. They nearly always require an observer on the ground to direct their attack

FORWARD OBSERVERS

The men on the ground who direct supporting fire require special training. They have to know how to operate the communication equipment that links them to the firing asset, whether it is an artillery battery or an airborne aircraft. They have to have an understanding both of the capabilities of the fire support system and the needs of the ground unit being supported. And finally, they need to know how to read a map.

This last point may sound frivolous, but it is not. Reading a high-

way map while motoring from Chicago to Detroit is comparatively simple; looking at a relief map and orienting your own position on it from visible landmarks is another story altogether. The average soldier cannot call for supporting fire because the average soldier, in even the best of armies, cannot locate his position or that of the enemy with certainty on a map. (This is sometimes a skill which young infantry officers find difficult to master as well, and many lieutenants welcome the company of a forward observer when moving cross country. The FOs always know where you are.)

The system of supporting fires depends on the competence of the FO and a secure communication link back to the fire support system. If the FO can be eliminated, or the communication link broken, the most powerful artillery systems are rendered impotent. In fact, this is exactly what happened to the Iraqi artillery during the war. While a great many guns were knocked out by the air attacks, those that were

left fired only sporadically and never very accurately. This was so because their FOs were scattered and their communications disrupted. Without target information, they were helpless.

THE NEW FO

New tools are making the FO's job easier. Among these tools are artillery fire-control computers, counterbattery radar, land navigation systems, and laser designators.

Fire control computers speed artillery response time considerably. An FO with a terminal linked to an artillery fire direction center (FDC) can type in the coordinates of the target and the FDC computer will calculate elevation, deflection, and charge and fuse settings for the guns almost instantaneously. All that is required is a load-and-fire command from the battery.

Counterbattery radars make it possible for the artillery battery itself to locate enemy indirect fire assets and fire back fairly quickly. This saves the FO from having to attempt difficult, and generally inaccurate, sound and flash ranging.

Land navigation systems increasingly allow gunners and FOs to communicate with each other with greater assurance of their own locations. That is critical to delivering accurate fire support.

Finally, lasers have the possibility of turning any soldier into an FO. Many modern smart munitions home on laser reflections. Once the round is in the air and

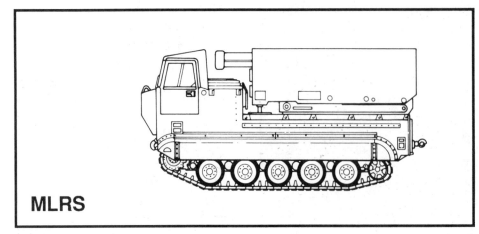

MLRS

coming down in the general area, all the soldier has to do is point the laser and pull the trigger.

TYPES OF ARTILLERY

There are two general types of artillery currently in use: tube artillery and rockets. Tube artillery refers to anything with a gun "tube," including mortars, howitzers, and long-range guns. All of them throw a ballistic projectile which explodes on contact.

Rockets, on the other hand, launch a self-propelled round which travels to the target. Traditionally, rocket artillery has been less accurate than tube artillery, but this is changing dramatically with modern rocket systems.

The advantages of rockets in the past were the low cost and relatively low sophistication of the launch system, and the ability to "salvo" large numbers of rockets from a single launcher, thus suddenly saturating a target with large numbers of rounds. The disadvantages were the larger bulk and cost of the ammunition, low accuracy, and long reload times.

Modern rockets can still fire salvos, but rely on fewer shots from more accurate launchers. Their principal advantage is that they can carry very large warheads. These are usually filled with submunitions: hundreds of small grenades or mines capable of killing infantry and damaging even

armored vehicles.

Tube artillery retains the advantage of relatively inexpensive and compact rounds. Large quantities of ammunition can be carried with the gun, enabling it to keep up a sustained fire over a longer period of time. A balanced allocation of fire support assets includes both types of artillery.

HELICOPTERS

Originally used in World War II for search-and-rescue missions, helicopters have grown into potent battlefield assets. Present-day helicopters are broadly broken into four categories: utility, cargo, observation, and attack.

Utility and cargo helicopters differ more in degree than type. Both can carry cargo and troops. Cargo choppers are big enough to carry heavy loads, but are not agile enough to carry troops into a hot assault landing. Utility choppers are.

Observation helicopters are the aerial scouts of modern aviation units. They seek out the enemy and then call in the heavies—the attack helicopters.

Attack helicopters are armed with a mixture of automatic cannons (usually 20mm or 25mm), free-flight rockets, and guided antitank missiles. Most antitank missiles are wire-guided, but a few are radio- or laser-guided. The TOW-II missiles on the army and marine Cobra attack helicopters are wire-guided, for example.

The Hellfire missiles on the new AH-64, on the other hand, home on laser reflection. The Apache has its own laser in a chin mount and can paint its own target. Alternatively, an accompanying observation helicopter can paint the target for the Apache, which then just has to "pop up," fire, and drop back behind cover. Since the observation helicopter is small and agile, it is comparatively safe from enemy observation.

US attack helicopters usually work in pairs, supported by one or two observation helicopters. One of the interesting surrender incidents happened before the start of the ground war when a pair of AH-64 attack helicopters, supported by two OH-58 observation helicopters, began systematically destroying the squad bunkers in an Iraqi battalion fort. After 13 bunkers had been destroyed, the survivors of the Iraqi battalion, about 400 men, surrendered to the four helicopters. Additional cargo helicopters had to be brought in to lift the EPWs out.

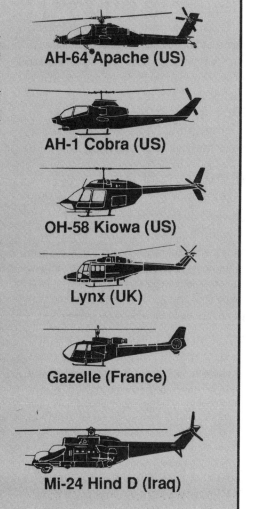

AH-64 Apache (US)

AH-1 Cobra (US)

OH-58 Kiowa (US)

Lynx (UK)

Gazelle (France)

Mi-24 Hind D (Iraq)

THE NATURE OF CONTEMPORARY AIR POWER

Although much press attention during the first month of Operation Desert Storm focused on smart weapons and "The Nintendo War," much of the air war would have seemed familiar to an aviator in the First World War, World War II or Vietnam. While there have been revolutionary changes in the tools of air power, the aviators who use those tools and the uses to which they are put have changed relatively little.

THE USES OF AIR POWER

In any war, air power can be used against three centers of enemy power. Air power can fight the enemy's air power, it can attack enemy surface (army and naval) forces, and it can bomb targets that will reduce an enemy's ability and/or will to sustain combat. (See following pages.)

ELEMENTS OF AIR POWER

While the most obvious element of air power may be aircraft dropping bombs, sometimes the "nonlethal" elements of air power have the greatest impact. Air power can be divided into three categories; forces that can be used with lethal effect directly against the enemy (combat forces), forces that increase the combat effectiveness of friendly air, sea, and land forces and degrade the combat effectiveness of enemy forces (what the US Air Force calls *enhancing forces* and the US Army calls *combat support*), and forces that sustain friendly air forces (support forces).

Combat Forces

Fighters: Fighters are built to kill other fighters; if they can do that they can easily destroy attack, bomber, and support aircraft. A high top speed is useful for intercepts, but more importantly fighters must be maneuverable and have good acceleration, to regain speed after maneuvers. Fighters also need sensors (radar, infrared, etc.) to find their prey and should be difficult to acquire themselves. Most fighters are single seat—a second crew member would add weight, reducing maneuverability and acceleration, and would require a larger, easier to see airframe.

Attack Aircraft: Attack aircraft engage surface forces. When armies and fleets fought only during the day and usually in good weather, attack aircraft only needed to fight during the day and in good weather. As more and more armies and fleet acquire night/all-weather capabilities, attack aircraft must also acquire such capabilities. Also, attack aircraft are more difficult to see and shoot down at night. The ability to accurately hit targets is important both for tactical effectiveness and to avoid losses to friendly forces.

The Multirole Combat Aircraft—Fighter/Attack: As air campaigns progress, commanders have varying needs for different types of aircraft. Hence, there has long been a desire for multirole aircraft. Some analysts also saw multirole aircraft as a way to save money. In time, an expensive lesson was learned: Aircraft designed to do many different things are very expensive and can't do anything well. But the desire for flexibility and cost savings remained. One approach was to design aircraft to perform two roles requiring similar attributes. Several types of fighter/attack aircraft have been built. After air supremacy is achieved, these "swing fighters" can turn to ground attack. However, these aircraft still cost more than a specialized aircraft and probably perform neither mission quite as well.

Bomber: Bombers tend to attack fixed targets. Their targets tend to be deeper in enemy territory, so range is more important, and at least two crew members are imperative as the concentration required by one crew member over hostile territory for extended periods bumps up against another biological barrier. Night/all-weather attack ability is useful in that this increases their survivability. Being difficult to detect (stealthy) is also important. The ability to accurately hit their targets is important both for military effectiveness and to limit civilian casualties. Since a limited number of missions will be flown in a day (probably one) a larger bomb load is desirable.

Force Enhancement/Combat Support Forces

These forces are commonly referred to as force multipliers, as they do not destroy enemy forces or sustainment capabilities themselves—they multiply the effectiveness of friendly forces that do and decrease the effectiveness of hostile forces. These forces include:

Reconnaissance: Reconnaissance aircraft let air, sea, and land commanders know where the enemy is (and is not). Accurate reconnaissance can make attacks more effective by identifying an enemy's most vulnerable points. Reconnaissance can also reduce friendly losses by identifying threats, permitting them to be avoided or countered.

Surveillance and Control: While reconnaissance aircraft support sound planning for future actions, surveillance and control aircraft help air, land, and sea forces fight more effectively—*now*. Powerful airborne sensors (usually radars) observe the battle area and controllers pass this information to air, sea, and land forces. Surveillance and control aircraft tend to be large in order to accommodate large sensors and several controllers.

Electronic Combat: Electronic combat can reduce the effectiveness of enemy forces by degrading their sensors or jamming their communications. Electronic combat can also increase the effectiveness of friendly forces by locating enemy transmitters that can then be avoided or attacked.

Airlift: The important role of airlift in strategic mobility has already been discussed. Airlift can also provide critical mobility during battles; both for friendly forces and supplies. Transports tend to have high wings so the fuselage can be relatively close to the ground, making loading and unloading quick and easy.

Aerial Refueling: Aerial tankers extend the range and capabilities of combat and force enhancement aircraft. For example, fighters can refuel while remaining airborne—ready to intercept hostile aircraft. Aerial tankers are usually

adapted transports or bombers.

Support Forces

Support forces include the aircraft mechanics that literally "keep 'em flying"—the munitions troops that arm the aircraft, the doctors, cooks, supply clerks, chaplains, and all the others that make air power function. For each air force member who flies there are typically 20 members who work on the ground.

THE LEGENDARY HERK

While it is generally true that an aircraft designed for a specific task tends to out-perform one designed for multiple roles there are exceptions to every rule. During the venerable C-130 tactical transport's long career, it has done it all:

Attack: Descended from "Puff the Magic Dragon," the Vietnam-era airborne gun platform, today's AC-130 is equipped with sophisticated sensors and several heavy weapons making it an effective weapon around the clock and in all weather.

Bombardment: The largest bomb used during Desert Storm was the "Daisy Cutter." Developed during Vietnam to clear landing zones for helicopters in dense jungle, it was used in Kuwait to clear minefields. It can only be delivered by the C-130.

Fighter: Okay, this is a bit of a stretch, but the AC-130's guns are effective against helicopters, and the USAF is actively considering mounting air-to-air missiles on some C-130s for self-protection.

Reconnaissance: The AC-130's sensors can collect a lot of information.

Surveillance and Control: The USAF has used the C-130 as a airborne command post and some countries have showed an interest in mounting surveillance radars in a C-130.

Electronic Warfare: The EC-130 is one of the United States' most capable electronic warfare aircraft, although it is prudent to keep it over friendly airspace.

Aerial Tanker: The KC-130 is one of the more popular models of aerial refueler.

Aviation Engineer: No, the C-130 does not build airfields, but specially modified Herks have demonstrated the ability to turn a section of highway or a dry lake bed into an air base. The C-130s land minutes before the combat aircraft they are to rearm. Maintenance troops emerge from the C-130s to refuel the combat aircraft with fuel from one C-130 while munitions from the other C-130 are used to rearm the combat aircraft.

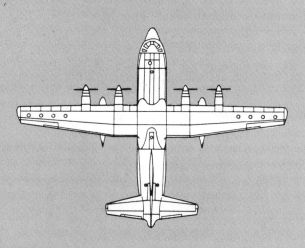

THE BATTLE FOR AIR SUPERIORITY
CONTROL OF THE AIR

When the words *air superiority* are used, the image that comes to mind is that of the ace and the aerial dogfight. While air superiority has been won and maintained through aerial combat, there have been many routes to control of the air. What exactly is air superiority, why is it so important, and, how is it achieved?

LEVELS OF AIRSPACE CONTROL

While most people talk about air superiority, the military speaks of *controlling airspace*. Control may be throughout the theater or local, and exists in several degrees:

Contested Air Control: If air control is contested throughout the theater both sides must fight to do what they want in the air.

Air Superiority: If one side wins most of the local fights for air superiority, that side is said to have general air superiority. That side would still escort important missions and maintain its air defenses as the enemy could still gain local air superiority in some places.

Air Supremacy: If one side gains air supremacy, the fight is over. Escorts can be eliminated and "swing fighters" can now swing to attacking ground forces.

AIR CONTROL'S VALUE

There is no question control of the air is valuable. Even most armies and navies agree the first priority in war is to ensure control of the air above friendly forces. Control of the air prevents enemy air attacks on friendly strategic centers. It also makes the enemy blind.

THE AIR BATTLE

Today, air battles are no more du-els between individual fighters than ground battles are duels between individual tanks; it can happen, but it is a small and somewhat rare part of a much bigger picture.

Air combat occurs for a reason. One side enters the airspace of its enemy to accomplish some task and the enemy tries to stop them. Their clash defines the modern air battle.

The Integrated Air Defense

The integrated air defense system consists of sensors to see what is happening, a command element to decide how to respond, forces with which to respond, and communications to tie all the above together. The defending air commander has three types of forces to respond with: antiaircraft artillery (AAA), surface-to-air missiles (SAMs), and his own aircraft, interceptors, and fighters.

Each has advantages and disadvantages:

Antiaircraft Artillery

+ Least expensive, many can be bought
+ Can be camouflaged and hardened
+ Shells can't be defeated by countermeasures
- Shortest range
- Fights from where it is when hostile aircraft spotted
- Hence, attackers can usually fly around or over it

Surface-to-Air Missiles

+ Less expensive than aircraft
+ Can be camouflaged and hardened
+ Much longer range than AAA
- Fights from where it is when hostile aircraft spotted
- Attacker can often fly around SAMs, especially at low altitudes
- SAMs guide on radar or heat; attacking aircraft can confuse guidance

Defending Aircraft

+ Can be moved to intercept attackers
+ Even if attacking aircraft confuse guidance of the defending aircraft's missiles, defender can still use gun
+ May be able to avoid fight if attacking aircraft is too strongly escorted
- Most expensive form of defense
- Some aircraft have trouble seeing enemy aircraft during night/bad weather or close to the ground
- Attacks on other parts of the air defense system can keep defending aircraft out of the fight.

An integrated air defense system blends these options to maximize the strengths of each and minimize their weaknesses.

The Force Package

To get through this integrated defense, an attacker has two basic options: avoid or overcome.

The attacking air forces could try to avoid enemy defenses. Stealth aircraft seek to avoid detection. Standoff weapons seek to keep attacking aircraft beyond the range of AAA around targets.

The other option is to overcome the defenses. The basic way this is done is the force package:

Force Package Components

Mission Aircraft: Usually the bomb carriers, their mission is the reason the force package was formed.

Fighter Escort: These fighters protect the rest of the package from the defending fighters.

Weasel Escort: These fighters protect the rest of the package from SAMs.

EW Aircraft: Their job is to *dis*integrate the enemy's integrated air defense system, keep the parts from seeing what is happening and talking to each other, and perhaps interfering with the guidance of individual defending weapons.

When the force package meets the integrated air defense, an air battle occurs. If the force package achieves surprise, or the electronic warfare aircraft is successful, or the defenders decide the escort is too strong to attack, no air combat may take place. If defending fighters close with the force package, classic dogfights may result.

AIR COMBAT

During World War I, most pilots that were shot down never saw the man who killed them. If the one side has a working surveillance and control system and the other side either has not or is beyond its range, the side without the system is at a tremendous disadvantage. For example, if the defender has such a system and the attacker does not, defending fighters could be directed to approach a force package from behind and below. Pilots of every nation are taught to "Check 6," or look behind themselves frequently, but with luck the first indication a force package may have that it is under attack is when the first aircraft explodes.

In the final analysis, who wins an air to air fight? There are several factors:

● Numbers count—not the number of aircraft in an inventory but the number ready to fight air to air where the fight takes place. An aircraft that can fly several times in a day (high sortie rate) is a tremendous advantage.

● How good the aircraft is suited for air-to-air combat matters.

● Armaments count—an aircraft without a radar missile is at a tremendous disadvantage to an aircraft that does. A heat-seeking missile that can shoot an enemy "in the face" has a tremendous advantage over an aircraft that must maneuver to a location behind its target to fire.

● Support counts—the pilot with information from a control system has a tremendous advantage over an opponent whose surveillance and control system has been jammed or destroyed.

● Finally, the man still counts—the most. Enough flying time every month, realistic simulators, dissimilar air combat training all play a part. But in the final analysis, the craft is but the instrument and the training—the coaching. It all comes down to a man willing to bet his life and good enough to win.

THE CAMPAIGN FOR AIR CONTROL

While a strong escort may allow a particular mission to get through, it is unlikely that a series of air-to-air battles will result in one side gaining decisive control of the air. If either side is losing too many aircraft, that side can avoid combat until it has licked its wounds. To gain air control it is usually necessary to aggressively attack all elements of an enemy's integrated air defense.

The objective is to *dis*integrate the enemy's integrated air defenses and destroy it piece by piece. Weasels attack enemy radars to blind the system. Force packages attack command and communication sights. Weasels hunt down and kill SAM batteries or the SAMs stay turned off to avoid destruction. Force packages attack air bases.

THE INDIRECT APPROACH

Just as air forces can be used to attack the sustainment of ground forces to reduce their effectiveness, a campaign for air supremacy can be assisted by attacks on the sustain-

ment of enemy air forces. These attacks can come from the air, sea, or land. During World War II, the Allies' efforts to gain air supremacy over Germany was greatly assisted by the destruction of its petrochemical industry by US bombers. The *Luftwaffe* did not have the fuel to train new pilots or even for current pilots to fly very much. When the Red Army captured the Rumanian oil fields, the last trickle of aviation fuel was cut off. Similarly, flight training and most combat flying in Japan was stopped by the US Navy's destruction of the Japanese merchant marine. Because of this loss, the Japanese had no way to transport their fuel from its source, what is today Indonesia.

THE ACE FACTOR

Throughout the history of air power the large majority of air to air victories have gone to a small percentage of the pilots. These "aces" seem to come from all nations and all walks of life. It is difficult to say what makes a pilot an ace, but it's easy to recognize when a pilot has "the right stuff." Although technology helps an ace, an inferior aircraft will frequently defeat an average pilot in a better craft. The fact that the Coalition suffered zero air-to-air losses at the hands of the Iraqis may be due more to the speed and effectiveness of the Coalition's campaign for air supremacy than the fighting qualities of Iraqi airmen.

STRATEGIC AIR OFFENSIVE

When military airmen talk of "strategic air offensive" they are referring to a campaign against targets vital to an enemy's ability and will to sustain a war. Prior to the development of modern air warfare, however, it was usually necessary to fight through the enemy's army or fleet to reach its vital centers.

Air power allowed vital centers to be attacked directly—attacked but not captured. When an "all clear" is sounded after a raid, the enemy still possesses the target. The enemy's usual response is to both repair and "adapt" the target. Hence, a strategic air offensive is a race between the attackers attempting to destroy faster than the defenders can rebuild.

STRATEGIC OPTIONS: WHAT TO BOMB

Any strategic air campaign has only so many aircraft available. On the other hand, there is likely to be a great number of potential targets. One of the most frequently made mistakes by air commanders is to try to hit so many targets that they are all hit too lightly and infrequently. How are targets selected?

To say that target selection should be driven by the overall theater campaign plain is just the beginning of an answer.

Much of the rest of the answer concerns a practical consideration of the capabilities and limitations of both the attacking aircraft and the defenders. It usually makes little sense to bomb a bridge at a location where a river can be easily forded. No matter how important a bunker is, if it is too hard to destroy, it makes little sense to try. Some industrial sites, like ball bearing plants, are inherently easy to disperse and harden.

Others, such as oil refineries, are very difficult to harden, impossible to disperse, and very slow to repair.

When you combine the importance of an effect to the overall campaign with the relative difficulty of achieving the required effect, you are close to a basis for selecting targets. The principal remaining considerations are political. The political fallout of accidental civilian casualties, our responsibility to future generations to preserve historical sites, and requirements of international law all have an appropriate role to play in target selection.

TYPES OF TARGETS

Command, Control and Communications (C³): Attacks on C³ targets have their greatest effect immediately after the attack. In time, old communications links are restored and new ones are devised. Hence, C³ attacks are most effective when they take place just as friendly forces start doing something new. The attacks will delay the enemy's reaction to your new action. Attacks when there is no need for the enemy's leadership to issue new orders may simply make it harder to disrupt communications when it will do some good.

War Production: This has been a common target for strategic offensives, but its effectiveness has varied. Toward the end of World War II many war production sights were so well dispersed, camouflaged and hardened that attacks

had little effect. On the other hand, Iraqi chemical and biological weapons plants appear to have been easy to destroy and impossible for the Iraqis to repair.

"Scientific" Sites: A new weapon can dramatically change the military landscape. Attacks on research-and-development sights that delay the adverse effect of new weapons can be very important. The destruction of Iraqis nuclear weapons program illustrated not only air power's ability to bypass surface forces to attack vital centers, but also to directly achieve what many believed to be one of the United States' unstated war aims.

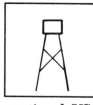
Oil: The dramatic effect of the Allied destruction of Nazi Germany's petrochemical industry has already been mentioned. US airmen hoped attacks on North Vietnam's oil storage facilities would have equally dramatic effects. However, the North Vietnamese got their fuel from allies and dispersed its storage in mostly small quantities in mostly residential areas.

Interdiction: Interdiction is an attack on an enemy's transportation system. Interdiction can hinder the flow of materials to factories or disrupt the flow of materials to armed forces.

The effectiveness of interdiction varies radically with geographic and weather conditions, as well as with the overall military situation. To interdict movement it must be observed. Interdiction over flat surfaces void of vegetation (such as deserts and oceans) tends to be far more effective than interdiction over triple-canopy jungle in mountains (the Ho Chi Minh Trail, for example). Heavy mechanized forces on the attack are far more vulnerable to interdiction than a guerrilla force that lives off the land.

FINDING
STRATEGIC TARGETS

(See the map on page 101.) When military briefers did not immediately know the effects of Desert Storm's initial air strikes, some criticized America's recon satellites. "After all," the arguments went, "if these things can read a license plate number from orbit, why don't we know the effects of these attacks?"

The truth of the matter is those "national assets" were designed for strategic reconnaissance, finding targets for strategic offensives. The type of reconnaissance needed for bomb damage assessment (BDA) and for keeping track of mobile surface forces is tactical reconnaissance and is best handled by aircraft that a commander can send where and when he needs information.

The movement of satellites is governed by the law of gravity. If, at the altitude and orbit they work best at, they overfly a particular spot on the earth every other day, there is not much that can be done. All such satellites carry some fuel, primarily to keep their attitude steady so they will function properly. This fuel can be used to adjust a satellite's orbit, but at the cost of reducing its useful life in orbit.

Finding strategic targets and developing information on them is truly a comprehensive intelligence operation. Some information is contained in "open" sources like phonebooks. In a country like Iraq, where many facilities were built by foreign firms, the prints of a facility may actually be available. Signals Intelligence (SIGINT) may be able indicate the use of a facility by the information going to and from it.

BOMBING
THE STRATEGIC TARGET

While criteria for target selection has evolved and assets for target location have gone into orbit, the most impressive changes have taken place in how targets are being bombed. Operation Desert Storm will long be remembered as "The Nintendo War" for the impressive films of the smart weapons. The implications of these films are even more impressive.

Even before World War II, the US Army Air Force advocated precision strategic bombing, both for reasons of military effectiveness and due to a humanitarian desire to minimize civilian casualties. The trouble was their precision bombing was not very precise. B-17s flew higher than expected to reduce the effectiveness of enemy AAA. The AAA still threw off their aim, as did the winds, as the bombs fell. The B-17 would fly 4500 sorties to drop the equivalent 9000 2000-pound bombs to destroy one target. If the target was located in a civilian area, the loss of innocent life could be high.

By the time of the Vietnam War, technology had improved but the effect of winds was still impossible to predict with certainty. What had required 4500 sorties now required "only" 95, and 190 2000-pound bombs. Most bombs were still missing their targets, so if the target was in a populated area it would be off limits for attack.

With new smart bombs, one bomb destroys one target. Winds are no longer a serious problem because if the bomb is being blown off its path to the target it will correct itself. Targets can be attacked in populated areas with the assurance that damage will be limited to essentially what was aimed at.

THE F-117

The F-117 achieved results completely out of proportion to its numbers. Comprising less than 5% of the Coalition's air strength, it was responsible for over a third of the attacks on strategic targets. Its effectiveness is even more impressive because other aircraft required force packages (fighter escort, SAM suppression, etc.), at least until air supremacy was achieved, while the F-117A went in alone. Add to this the facts that F-117As attacked the most heavily defended targets deep in Iraqi territory and not one plane or pilot was lost.

How did the F-117A do it? While the exact technical techniques of stealth are classified, the basic principle is simple: You know by looking at the world around you that whether or not you can see something depends upon how far away it is and how "visible" it is.

Stealth technology makes the F-117A much harder for radar to see. Additionally, the F-117A makes sure it never gets close enough to an enemy radar to be detected.

It does this in two ways. It flies between the big, powerful radars that search for incoming aircraft. Radars controlling SAMs near its target are smaller, so the F-117A can get closer safely. To avoid getting close enough to be seen, it uses smart standoff weapons. The very weapons that give the F-117A its amazing accuracy also increase its survivability. Best of all, the F-117A carries two 2000-pound smart bombs, so instead of talking about how many sorties are needed to destroy one target, two targets are destroyed per sortie.

AIR ATTACKS ON SURFACE FORCES

The military situation confronting Coalition leaders has been described as an air power advocate's dream come true. A large army with tanks and other big, easy-to-see pieces of equipment deployed on a flat, barren waste with nothing to hide behind. On the way, the visibility was supposed to be unlimited. But, in many ways the outcome of Desert Storm exceeded the expectations of the most optimistic air power advocate.

Ironically, the operation also revealed a shortcoming of air power, not trivial in its impact and heretofore unreported. Although one group of Iraqi soldiers did succeed in surrendering to an A-10 Thunderbolt, it was not generally possible for the Iraqis to surrender to attacking aircraft. There are growing indications that many Iraqis would have welcomed an earlier opportunity to surrender.

Many more tons of bombs were dropped during the eight years of American air involvement in Vietnam than the six weeks of Desert Storm and produced much less effect. What made air attack so devastating during Desert Storm? Put simply, the geography and climate was more favorable, the technology had improved, and Coalition doctrine was more effective. But there are final factors that may be the most important of all.

GEOGRAPHY AND CLIMATE

It's been said many times, but it bears repeating: It is a lot easier to see the enemy on a flat desert than through a three-canopy jungle turned sideways by a mountainside. For 50 years the concept that there is good tank country (plains and deserts) and bad tank country (swamps and cities) has been ac-cepted wisdom in the worlds militaries. Yet it seems strange to talk about good aircraft country.

While aircraft fly across a mile of any terrain at precisely the same speed, the terrain becomes very relevant when it comes to combat. The less natural opportunity for surface forces to hide, the more effective air power can be. Air power is probably most effective at sea where there is no verification or ridgelines. The flat, barren wastes of Kuwait are a close second.

Climate and weather also play an important part. Air attack on surface forces can be likened to a race between the destructive powers of the attacker and the recuperative abilities of the defender. Any pause caused by weather gives defenders time to recover and take measures to reduce the effectiveness of future attacks. Many Coalition aircraft were day/good-weather only. The ability of thise aircraft known as "all weather" to fight in poor weather conditions varies greatly. In truly dreadful weather few aircraft are effective.

INTO THE NIGHT, THE TECHNOLOGY GETS BETTER

Following World War II, the commander of a German Panzer Corps complained that trying to fight when the Allies had air supremacy was like playing chess against someone who had three moves for every one move of yours. The Allies could move their forces morning, noon and night while he could only move his forces under cover of darkness. Technological advances have taken away even this one move from the side that has lost control of the air.

Devices to help pilots attack at night are collectively called electro-optic (EO) devices. The most effective night attack technology is the forward-looking infrared (FLIR). Aircraft like the USAF F-111F and the US Navy/US Marines A-6E first use their radars to find the approximate location of the attack. As the aircraft approach the target, the FLIR is switched on. The FLIR sees the relative heat of items in its field of view and displays it on a screen. It is important that the FLIR is pointed in approximately the right direction to start with because the field of view of the FLIR has been likened to "looking down a straw." The US Air Force's F-111F does have a zoom feature on its FLIR, but even in the "wide" angle setting it's been described as "looking down a big straw."

While effective, the US Air Force F-111Fs, and to a lesser degree the US Navy's A-6Es, tend to attack strategic targets, and both services have been working on improving the night-attack capabilities of their aircraft that tend to attack surface forces. The newer Navy/Marine Corps F/A-18s have some night-attack capabilities. The US Air Force decided to go with a "pod" system called the low-altitude navigation and targeting infrared system (Lantern). The Lantern system fits into two fairly small streamlined pods that can be mounted on an aircraft prior to night attacks. The pods can then be removed prior to daylight operations to reduce the weight of the aircraft and avoid being lost or damaged if the aircraft is hit. One Lantern pod is a truly wide-angle FLIR that allows the pilot to fly at low levels at night. As the radar does not have to be used, there is less chance that an enemy will know an attack is coming. The pod contains the traditional "look through a straw" targeting FLIR. Unfortunately, Lantern had not been in production for long when Operation Desert Shield began and it is unclear if crew training was sufficiently far enough along for the system's use in Desert Storm.

Another method of night attack involves the use of night vision goggles. The pilot wears goggles that amplify existing light. Except for special cockpit lighting that is compatible with the goggles, there are no modifications to the aircraft. The system's only drawback is that it substantially reduces a pilot's depth perception; this is not a trivial drawback when flying at low levels. Still, it is used by pilots of the US Marines AV-8B Harrier vertical takeoff-and-landing jet and many helicopters and is spoken well of by those who use it.

One of the more interesting methods of night attack is employed by the USAF's A-10. The aircraft has no systems to see at night but it carries the Maverick missile that can have an imaging infrared seekerhead. This is a missile that can see at night, and what it sees is displayed in the A-10 cockpit. Of course, when all the missiles are fired the aircraft can no longer see ground targets, but then it is out of ammunition and doesn't need to anyway.

JOINT ATTACK

The quality of the synergism between air and surface forces has fluctuated. Usually lessons are learned the hard way in war, only to be forgotten in peace. Somehow during the last decade the United States has broken this pattern. US forces entered combat far better prepared to work as an air, land, and sea team than in any previous war in US history.

Part of the credit probably goes to the US Army. They developed a new doctrine called AirLand Battle. Despite air getting top billing, the doctrine did give ground forces the dominant role; it was never accepted by the US Air Force.

Still, it represented a huge step in the right direction and sparked continuing analysis of how land and air forces can best be used together.

Embarrassment may have also played a part. The confusion and difficulties of the services to talk to each other during the Grenada invasion are legendary. In fairness, most of the problems could be traced to the extraordinarily short time available for planning and conducting the operation. Still, the perception was created that the services could not work together. The US Armed Forces looked even worse after the near flawless synergism of air and land forces displayed by Israel in its move into southern Lebanon.

The next part of the story is a bit of "what came first, the chicken or the egg?" Both the US Congress and the US Armed Forces started to move toward greater "jointness," closer teamwork between the services. Congress passed the Goldwater-Nickols Act that increased the authority of the chairman of the Joint Chiefs of Staff and the commanders in chief (CinCs) of Unified Commands (commands like Central Command that include elements of several services). The service war colleges started increasing the proportion of "joint studies" in their curricula. The Pentagon and the Unified Commands began putting increased emphasis on planning and wargaming unified campaign plans.

CLOSE AIR SUPPORT/ CLOSE GROUND SUPPORT

The payoff for all these preparations can be seen on the battlefield. The principal concept of joint air/ground attack on a target was close air support. If it soj happened that some attack aircraft were available, the ground commander would decide where they would do the most good. In part due to the example of the Israelis, something that could be called close ground support of air operations has evolved. Ground force artillery would attack enemy antiair-

craft weapons. With the area now safer, aircraft might then attack enemy artillery before it could fire back at friendly artillery.

THE FINAL FACTORS

To paraphrase General George C. Kenny, few advantages in war are as valuable as being up against a dummy.

The Iraqi soldiers were no dummies. They would start smoky fires in cans on undamaged tanks to make Coalition pilots think the tank had already been destroyed. They would paint and make superficial repairs to destroyed tanks in the hope additional ordnance would be wasted on them. Finally, they had the good sense to surrender when the situation became hopeless.

Saddam Hussein put his army in an impossible position. He stopped his forces on terrain—an attack pilot's dream. Then he left them there long enough for US reconnaissance satellites to map every bunker. If he had moved forward in August he may have captured the air bases the Coalition needed to bring its air power to bear. If he withdrew, he would have at least saved his army. As any student of air power would agree, General Schwarzkopf's now famous assessment of Saddam Hussein's generalship was probably generous.

"As far as Saddam Hussein being a great military strategist, he is neither a strategist, nor is he schooled in the operational arts, nor is he a tactician, nor is he a general, nor is he a soldier. Other than that, he's a great military man, I want you to know that."

COALITION TANKS

M1A1

The M1A1 is the most advanced tank in the US arsenal, and is arguably the best tank in service in the world today. It uses Chobham armor, and the most recent version incorporates a mesh of ultra-hard depleted uranium in the armor to further increase protection. It is also one of the fastest tanks in service.

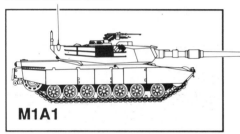

M1A1

Specifications
Weight: 65 tons
Road Speed: 72 kph
Gun: 120mm smoothbore
Fire Control: Laser range finder, ballistic computer, stabilized gun
Rounds Carried: 40
Armor: 600mm (1300mm versus HEAT warheads) '
In Service With: USA

M60A3 MBT

The M60 is a progressive development of the M48 medium tank. All versions of the M60 use the 105mm rifled gun, but the most recent versions include a ballistic computer and tank thermal sight (TTS). USMC M60s are equipped with reactive armor array (RAA) blocks which provides additional protection against HEAT warheads. Other Coalition forces using the M60 are not equipped with RAA.

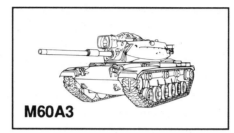

M60A3

Specifications
Weight: 51.5 tons
Road Speed: 48 kph
Gun: 105mm
Fire Control: Laser range finder, ballistic computer
Rounds Carried: 63
Armor: 250mm (500mm versus HEAT, USMC with RAA only)
In Service With: USMC, Saudi Arabia, Bahrain, Egypt

M-551 SHERIDAN AIRBORNE LIGHT TANK

Originally intended as a general-purpose reconnaissance vehicle, the Sheridan experienced continuous problems with its main armament, which consists of a gun capable of firing either a 152mm low-velocity round or a Shillelagh missile. In practice, the recoil generated by firing a conventional round often damages the missile guidance system, rendering the

M-551 Sheridan

launcher inoperative. Because of this and other problems it was phased out of general service, but still equips the airborne light tank battalion of the 82nd Airborne Division, and these were the first US tanks to arrive in Saudi Arabia.

Specifications
Weight: 16 tons
Road Speed: 65 kph
Gun: 152mm gun/launcher
Fire Control: Laser range finder
Rounds Carried: 20 cannon rounds, 10 Shillelagh missiles
Armor: 100mm
In Service With: US 82nd Airborne Division

AMX-30

The AMX-30, produced by France from the mid-1960s, was designed to emphasize speed and firepower over armor protection. For maximum protection, it adopted a 105mm gun optimized to fire HEAT rounds, as those were the best armor penetrators at that time. The passage of time has proven most of the AMX-30's design decisions to be wrong. Chobham and reactive armor have significantly reduced the value of HEAT warheads. New hyper velocity rounds are excellent penetrators, but the AMX-30's gun is not powerful enough to take full advantage of them. New power plant technology has increased the speed of most tanks to equal or better than that of the AMX-30. This leaves it a lightly armored tank of average speed and mediocre killing power. The improved AMX-30B2 version, in service with French forces in the theater, has a laser range finder and additional armor protection.

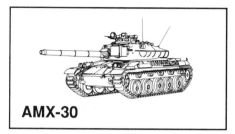
AMX-30

Specifications
Weight: 36 tons
Road Speed: 65 kph
Gun: 105mm rifled gun
Fire Control: Coincidence range finder (laser range finder on AMX-30B2)
Rounds Carried: 47
Armor: 150mm (180mm on AMX-30B2)
In Service With: Saudi Arabia, UAE, Qatar, France (B2)

CHIEFTAIN MK 5
When introduced the Chieftain had the thickest armor and most powerful gun of any tank in the world. It was also extremely slow, although the current production versions are better in that regard.

Chieftain Mk 5

Specifications
Weight: 55 tons
Road Speed: 48 kph
Gun: 120mm rifled gun
Fire Control: Laser range finder
Rounds Carried: 64
Armor: 400mm
In Service With: Oman, Kuwait

M-84
This is the Yugoslavian-produced version of the Soviet T-72 tank. Aside from the armored track skirts, the only visible difference from the Soviet T-72 is the presence of a wind sensor on the turret roof.

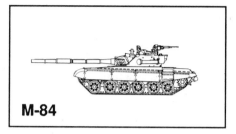
M-84

Specifications
Weight: 41 tons
Road Speed: 50 kph
Gun: 125mm smoothbore gun
Fire Control: Laser range finder, ballistic computer, stabilized gun
Rounds Carried: 40
Armor: 250mm
In Service With: Kuwait

CHALLENGER MBT
The Challenger has been a considerable disappointment in service due to problems with the main gun. The Challenger uses a modified version of the Chieftain's rifled 120mm gun which allows it to fire hyper-velocity APFSDS ammunition. However, the awkward placement of the fire-control equipment in the turret makes it difficult for the crew to effectively engage moving targets. This is a disadvantage in a tank duel, but would not matter much for long-range sniping.

Specifications
Weight: 62 tons
Road Speed: 60 kph
Gun: 120mm rifled gun
Fire Control: Laser range finder, ballistic computer, stabilized gun

Rounds Carried: 52
Armor: 500mm (800mm versus HEAT warheads)
In Service With: United Kingdom

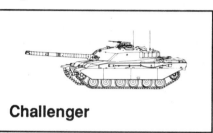
Challenger

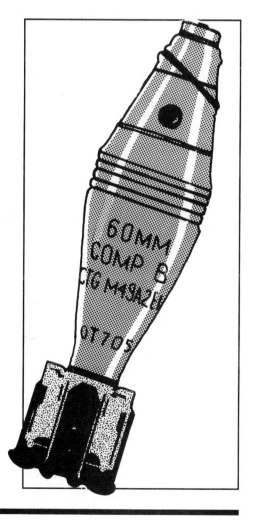

IRAQI TANKS

Although armor cannot win a battle by itself, armored fighting vehicles form the core of any offensive force on the modern battlefield, especially in largely open ground such as the Arabian Peninsula. The Iraqi armored forces were the best trained and led in their army and offered the only serious resistance to the Allied offensive.

T-54/55 MAIN BATTLE TANK

The T-54, and the slightly improved T-55, appeared in the 1950s. Despite their considerable age, they remain in service with armies worldwide in large numbers. Today they are badly outmatched in tank duels by almost any Allied tank.

Specifications

Weight: 36 tons
Road Speed: 48 kph
Gun: 100mm D-10T2S
Fire Control: Optic sights
Rounds Carried: 34 (T-54), 43 (T-55)
Armor: 200mm
Number on Hand: 1400

IMPROVED T-55 MAIN BATTLE TANK

The Iraqis have produced two improved versions of the T-55 tank. One of these, provisionally designated the T-55+, retains the 100mm gun of the original tank but adds an appliqué armor kit believed to have been purchased from China. This kit increases the armor basis of the tank by perhaps 150mm and gives it a distinctly angular, non-Soviet appearance.

The second version, sometimes referred to as the T-55Q, replaces the 100mm gun with a 125mm smoothbore gun, complete with autoloader and laser range finder. This is a locally manufactured copy of the Soviet gun system used on the T-72. Neither of these variants were encountered in large numbers.

Specifications

Weight: 36 tons (T-55Q), 40+ tons (T-55+)
Road Speed: 48 kph
Gun: 125mm smoothbore (T-55Q), 100mm D-10T2S (T-55+)
Fire Control: Laser range finder
Rounds Carried: 40 (T-55Q), 43 (T-55+)
Armor: 200mm (T-55Q), 350mm (T-55+)
Number on Hand: Few

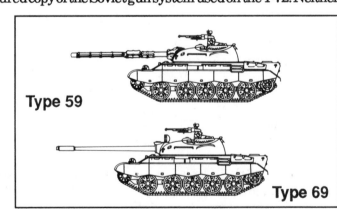

TYPE 59/69 MAIN BATTLE TANK

The Chinese Type 59 is an austere copy of the T-54, and lacks a number of "luxuries" (such as powered turret traverse) that most armies consider necessities. The Type 69 includes a laser range finder and a complete NBC protection system. Both the Type 59 and 69 have scalloped side skirts, making them visually distinct from the standard T-55. The Type 69 is a more modern version of the Type 59. All Type 59 tanks in Iraqi service have apparently been refitted with a 105mm tank gun and laser range finder, but the Type 69s apparently retained their Soviet 100mm guns.

Recent production examples of these tanks exported to other countries have shown signs of very poor quality control, including critical components such as the turret ring and traversing gears.

Specifications
Weight: 36 tons
Road Speed: 48 kph
Gun: 100mm D-10T2S (Type 69), 105mm L7 (Type 59)
Fire Control: Laser range finder
Rounds Carried: 34
Armor: 200mm
Number on Hand: 500 Type 59, 1000 Type 69

T-62 MAIN BATTLE TANK
The T-62 is a simple follow-on to the T-55. It uses a slightly modified turret to accept the more powerful U-5TS 115mm smoothbore, the first smoothbore tank gun adopted by the Soviets. Accuracy of this gun is better than the 100mm rifled gun of the T-54/55, but is still poor by modern standards. The T-62 forms the bulk of the "modern" tanks in Iraqi service. Relatively few T-62s were exported, even to Warsaw Pact nations, but most of those which were sent overseas were shipped to the Arab states in the early 1970s. Most Iraqi T-62s are concentrated in the elite Republican Guard divisions.

T-62

Specifications
Weight: 36.5 tons
Road Speed: 50 kph
Gun: 115mm U-5TS
Fire Control: Optic sights (some have laser RF retrofitted)
Rounds Carried: 40
Armor: 200mm
Number on Hand: 1000

T-72

T-72 MAIN BATTLE TANK
Although better than earlier Soviet tanks, the basic T-72 production model is poorly protected by contemporary standards, and the fact that the fuel and ammo are packed tightly together in the cramped hull makes a high percentage of hits catastrophic kills. Recognizing this failing, the Soviets have progressively increased the armor on later production versions of the T-72. The T-72M model has a visibly thicker hull and turret front. (The noticeable turret bulge in the front has led this variant to be nicknamed the "Dolly Parton" by US tankers.) This vehicle has estimated frontal protection equivalent to 350mm of armor plate.

The latest variant, the T-72M1, has even thicker turret armor (upping its protection to 400mm and earning it the nickname "Dolly Parton II"), appliqué armor on the turret roof, and a laser range finder.

A continuing problem in Soviet tank design for nearly 30 years has been disappointing main gun accuracy, and the T-72 continues that dubious tradition. Because of the high velocity and flat trajectory, accuracy is good out to 1500 meters but falls off drastically after that.

The majority of Iraq's T-72s are early production (T-72B) and export versions (T-72G). There are probably no more than 300 of the T-72M and T-72M1 versions on hand.

Specifications
Weight: 41 tons
Road Speed: 50 kph
Gun: 125mm
Fire Control: Laser range finder, stabilized gun system

Rounds Carried: 40
Armor: 250mm (350mm in T-72M, 400mm in T-72M1)
Number on Hand: 1000

TANK VS. TANK
THE RIVAL TANKS

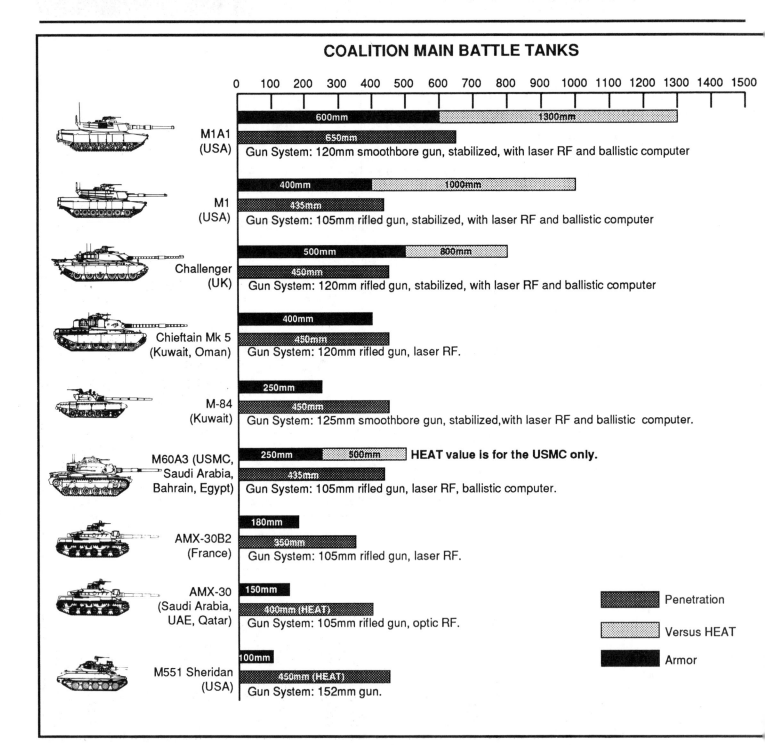

COALITION MAIN BATTLE TANKS

0 100 200 300 400 500 600 700 800 900 1000 1100 1200 1300 1400 1500

M1A1 (USA)
600mm
1300mm
650mm
Gun System: 120mm smoothbore gun, stabilized, with laser RF and ballistic computer

M1 (USA)
400mm
1000mm
435mm
Gun System: 105mm rifled gun, stabilized, with laser RF and ballistic computer

Challenger (UK)
500mm
800mm
450mm
Gun System: 120mm rifled gun, stabilized, with laser RF and ballistic computer

Chieftain Mk 5 (Kuwait, Oman)
400mm
450mm
Gun System: 120mm rifled gun, laser RF.

M-84 (Kuwait)
250mm
450mm
Gun System: 125mm smoothbore gun, stabilized, with laser RF and ballistic computer.

M60A3 (USMC, Saudi Arabia, Bahrain, Egypt)
250mm
500mm **HEAT value is for the USMC only.**
435mm
Gun System: 105mm rifled gun, laser RF, ballistic computer.

AMX-30B2 (France)
180mm
350mm
Gun System: 105mm rifled gun, laser RF.

AMX-30 (Saudi Arabia, UAE, Qatar)
150mm
400mm (HEAT)
Gun System: 105mm rifled gun, optic RF.

M551 Sheridan (USA)
100mm
450mm (HEAT)
Gun System: 152mm gun.

Penetration

Versus HEAT

Armor

The graphic below compares the capabilities of the principal tanks of the two sides, with particular emphasis on armor protection and main gun penetration, the two most important technical measures of combat performance. Penetration listed is for APFSDS ammunition except for those cases when the tank's standard antitank round is HEAT. These instances are labeled.

Hitting at long range is also critical when fighting in the desert. The gun system describes not only the gun, but also the range finder used. Laser range finders are superior to optic range finders. Ballistic computers also improve long-range accuracy. Stabilized guns can be fired accurately while the tank is moving; tanks without stabilized guns must halt to fire.

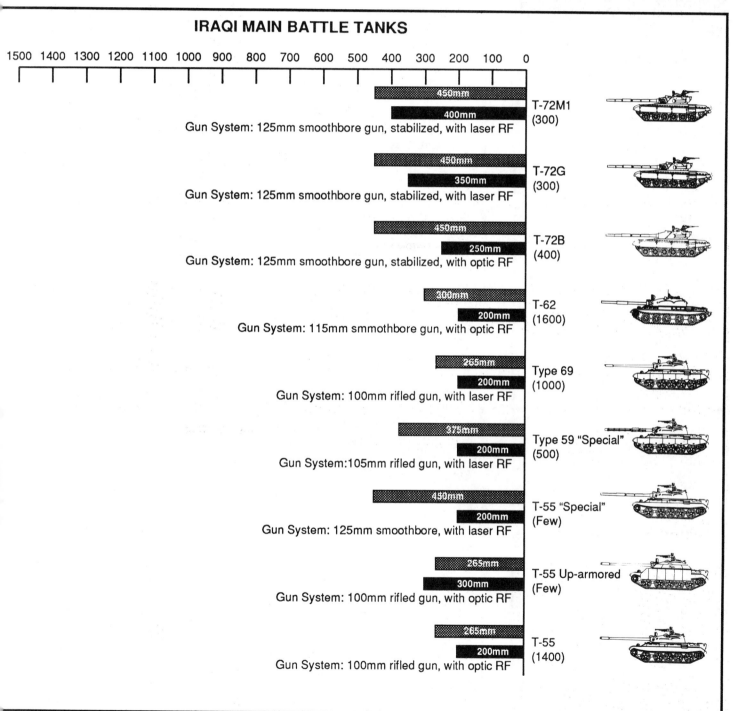

IRAQI MAIN BATTLE TANKS

| 1500 1400 1300 1200 1100 1000 900 800 700 600 500 400 300 200 100 0 |

T-72M1 (300)
450mm
400mm
Gun System: 125mm smoothbore gun, stabilized, with laser RF

T-72G (300)
450mm
350mm
Gun System: 125mm smoothbore gun, stabilized, with laser RF

T-72B (400)
450mm
250mm
Gun System: 125mm smoothbore gun, stabilized, with optic RF

T-62 (1600)
300mm
200mm
Gun System: 115mm smmothbore gun, with optic RF

Type 69 (1000)
265mm
200mm
Gun System: 100mm rifled gun, with laser RF

Type 59 "Special" (500)
375mm
200mm
Gun System:105mm rifled gun, with laser RF

T-55 "Special" (Few)
450mm
200mm
Gun System: 125mm smoothbore, with laser RF

T-55 Up-armored (Few)
265mm
300mm
Gun System: 100mm rifled gun, with optic RF

T-55 (1400)
265mm
200mm
Gun System: 100mm rifled gun, with optic RF

MODERN BUSHWACKERS
THE TANK KILLERS

It is often said that the best way to kill a tank is with another tank. Although that is probably true, it is not always possible. Infantry forces need means of their own to defend against tanks, since they can't always count on friendly armor being there when it's needed.

The solution is a mix of antitank

WHO USES WHAT?
Antitank
Guided Missiles
Hellfire: USA
TOW: Egypt, Morocco, Oman, Saudi Arabia, UAE, Bahrain
I-TOW: Kuwait
TOW II: USA
Milan: France, UK, Oman, Qatar, UAE, Egypt
Dragon: Morocco, USA, Saudi Arabia
AT-3 Sagger: Iraq, Syria
AT-4 Spigot: Iraq, Syria, Kuwait
HOT: France, Iraq, Kuwait, Qatar, Saudi Arabia, UAE
Swingfire: UK

Light Antitank Weapons
LRAC F1: France
Carl Gustav: UK, Kuwait, Qatar, Saudi Arabia, UAE
RPG-7: Syria, Egypt, Iraq
AT-4: USA
M72A1 LAW: Morocco, USA
LAW 80: UK

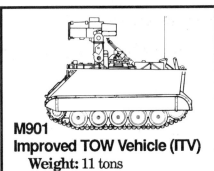

M901
Improved TOW Vehicle (ITV)
Weight: 11 tons
Armament: TOW-II
Used By: USA, Egypt, Kuwait

rocket launchers for close work and antitank missiles for long-range fire. Rocket launchers have to be light enough to be carried by the troopers when dismounted from their vehicles, and so weight places some upper limits on their performance.

Antitank missiles, on the other hand, can be carried by vehicles, and so can be much heavier. Missiles carried by infantry cannot be that heavy, though, so there are two schools of thought as to what the actual infantry platoon should use.

One school of thought favors a

Striker Antitank Vehicle
Weight: 8 tons
Armament: Swingfire
Used By: UK

heavy missile permanently mounted on the vehicle. Examples of this are the Bradley IFV with its TOW II or the Soviet BMP-2 with AT-5 Spandrel. (Kuwaiti BMP-2s are Czech-manufactured export versions fitted only with the AT-4.)

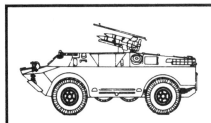

BRDM-2 Antitank Vehicle
Weight: 8 tons
Armament: AT-3 Sagger
Used By: Iraq

The other school of thought favors a missile light enough for the dismounted infantry to carry. The British and French both hold to this, and use the Milan. Because of weight limits, it has a shorter range than TOW. The French provide a mount on their AMX-10P IFV so that the Milan can be used as a vehicle weapon when the squad is mounted, and then taken off the vehicle when the squad dismounts.

The US has opted for an expensive, but effective, means of having it both ways. In addition to the vehicle-mounted TOW II launcher, the squad also has a man-portable Dragon launcher which is used when it dismounts.

Regardless of the solution adopted at the platoon and company level, most armies also provide additional antitank defense in the form of specialized antitank vehicles. These vehicles are usually armored personnel carriers or armored cars fitted with a long-range missile launcher. Instead of infantry, the vehicle carries a dozen or more reload missiles.

These specialized tank destroyers are usually formed as antitank companies at battalion or brigade level. The whole company can be assigned to cover critical parts of the front, but more often it is broken up into platoons and used to augment the defenses of

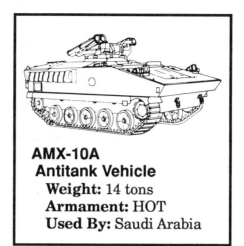

AMX-10A
Antitank Vehicle
Weight: 14 tons
Armament: HOT
Used By: Saudi Arabia

the maneuver companies.

In a US mechanized infantry battalion, for example, there are

four mechanized infantry companies (14 M2 Bradley IFVs each), and an antiarmor company (12 M901 Improved TOW vehicles). Some armies have a whole battalion of antitank vehicles in each division.

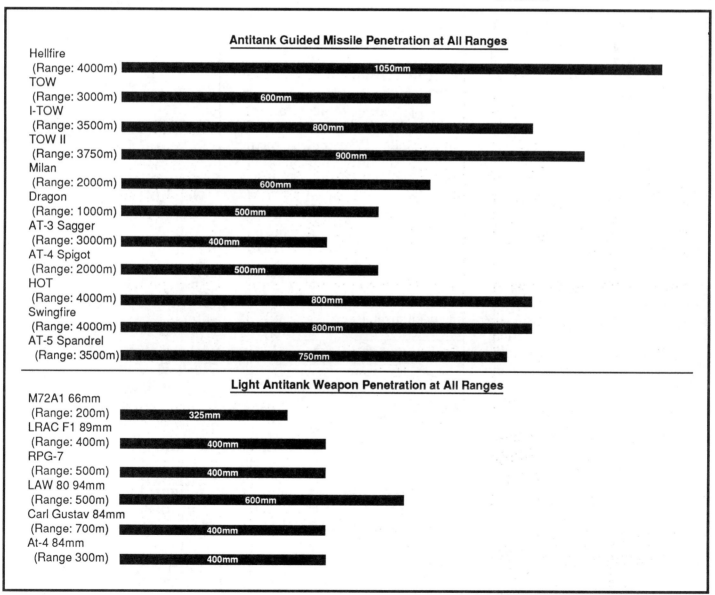

Antitank Guided Missile Penetration at All Ranges

Weapon	Penetration
Hellfire (Range: 4000m)	1050mm
TOW (Range: 3000m)	600mm
I-TOW (Range: 3500m)	800mm
TOW II (Range: 3750m)	900mm
Milan (Range: 2000m)	600mm
Dragon (Range: 1000m)	500mm
AT-3 Sagger (Range: 3000m)	400mm
AT-4 Spigot (Range: 2000m)	500mm
HOT (Range: 4000m)	800mm
Swingfire (Range: 4000m)	800mm
AT-5 Spandrel (Range: 3500m)	750mm

Light Antitank Weapon Penetration at All Ranges

Weapon	Penetration
M72A1 66mm (Range: 200m)	325mm
LRAC F1 89mm (Range: 400m)	400mm
RPG-7 (Range: 500m)	400mm
LAW 80 94mm (Range: 500m)	600mm
Carl Gustav 84mm (Range: 700m)	400mm
At-4 84mm (Range 300m)	400mm

BATTLE TAXIS AND CAVALRY CHARGERS
COALITION LIGHT AFVS

M113 APC

The M113 is one of the most widely used armored vehicles in history. Egyptian M-113s have additional appliqué armor which increases the protection to between 50 and 60mm.

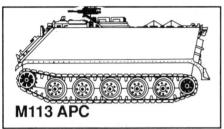
M113 APC

Specifications
Weight: 11 tons
Road Speed: 67.6 kph
Gun: 12.7mm machinegun
Troops: 11
Armor: 30mm
In Use With: Saudi Arabia, Kuwait, Egypt, Morocco

M2 BRADLEY IFV

The Bradley's side armor consists of two ¼-inch hard steel plates and an offset one-inch aluminum plate. The space between the plates provides extra protection against spaced charges. Overall, the equivalent protection against conventional rounds is the same as 30mm of steel. The later variant (M2A1) has 30mm of steel appliqué armor added to the front

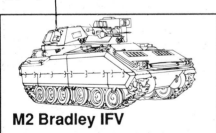
M2 Bradley IFV

and sides. Most vehicles with VII Corps are of the improved type.

Specifications
Weight: 22.59 tons
Speed: 66 kph
Gun: 25mm chaingun and TOW II launcher
Troops: 7
Armor: 30mm (M2), 60mm (M2A1)
In Use With: US Army

WARRIOR IFV

The United Kingdom was the last major power to adopt an infantry fighting vehicle, and some critics wonder if Warrior was worth the wait. It is not amphibious and, unlike virtually all other IFVs, it has neither an integral ASTGM launch system or provision for mounting the squad's launcher on the turret. This omission reduces the vehicle's effectiveness and flexibility. The notion of retrofitting a mount for the squad's Milan has been discussed.

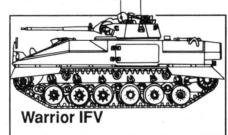
Warrior IFV

Specifications
Weight: 24 tons
Road Speed: 75 kph
Gun: 30mm Rarden
Troops: 7 or 8
Armor: 40-60mm
In Use With: United Kingdom

AMX-10P IFV

The turret has a mounting which can accept a Milan missile. Usually the squad has a Milan launcher which it will mount on the vehicle during an advance but will dismount when occupying defensive positions. Some AMX-10Ps in the region are used as SP mounts for HOT ATGM systems. It is a popular vehicle.

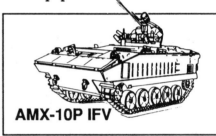
AMX-10P IFV

Specifications
Weight: 14.2 tons
Speed: 65 kph
Gun: 20mm
Troops: 8
Armor: 30mm
In Use With: France, Saudi Arabia, United Arab Emirates, Qatar

VAB (*VEHICULE DE L'AVANT BLINDÉ*) APC

A French-manufactured, light, wheeled APC used as a command vehicle or recon infantry transporter.

Specifications
Weight: 13 tons
Speed: 92 kph
Gun: 7.62mm
Troops: 10
Armor: 12mm
In Use With: France, Qatar

AMX-10RC (*ROUES CANON*) ARMORED CAR

Lightly armored and fast, the AMX-10RC is employed more as a light tank or tank destroyer than a recon vehicle. AMX-10RC units tend to perform more traditional cavalry functions, such as screening enemy positions, rapidly occupying and holding undefended or lightly defended ground, covering withdrawals, etc.

AMX-10RC Armored Car

Specifications
Weight: 15.8 tons
Speed: 85 kph
Gun: 105mm
Ammo: 38
Armor: 40mm
In Use With: France

SCORPION/SCIMITAR LIGHT RECON VEHICLE

The Scorpion and Scimitar are essentially identical vehicles, differing only in their armament. They are intended to operate together; Scorpion will engage heavier targets with HEAT rounds while Scimitar engages light AFVs with rapid cannon fire.

Scorpion/Scimitar

Specifications
Weight: 8 tons (Scorpion), 7.76 tonnes (Scimitar)
Road Speed: 80.5 kph
Gun: 76mm (Scorpion), 30mm (Scimitar)
Ammo: 40 76mm or 165 30mm
Armor: 45mm
Scorpion In Use With: United Kingdom, United Arab Emirates, Oman
Scimitar In Use With: United Kingdom

BMP-2 IFV

This is the improved version of the Soviet BMP-1. Principal visual differences include a larger two-man turret placed farther back on the chassis, a long-barreled autocannon in place of the shorter, thicker 73mm smoothbore, and a tubular missile launcher mounted on a pedestal in the center of the turret instead of an exposed missile on a launch rail over the gun tube.

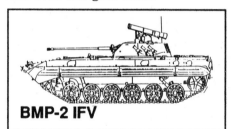

BMP-2 IFV

Specifications
Weight: 14 tons
Speed: 70 kph
Gun: 30mm
Missile: AT-4
Ammo: 200 30mm, 3 AT-4 missiles
Troops: 7
Armor: 15-20mm
In Use With: Kuwait

AAV-7A1 ARMORED AMPHIBIOUS TROOP CARRIER

Originally designated the LVTP-

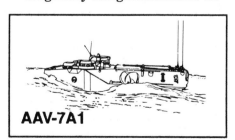

AAV-7A1

7, this is a slightly improved version. Over 800 are in service worldwide, and over half of these are in or on their way to the Persian Gulf, enough to lift almost all of the Marine infantry units present.

Specifications
Weight: 23 tons
Speed: 64 kph
Gun: 12.7mm machinegun
Troops: 25
Armor: 30mm+
In Use With: USMC

LAV-25 IFV

Each USMC division has a light armored assault battalion with over 100 LAV-25s. These are allocated by company to individual Marine expeditionary brigades, with each having an average of about 50 vehicles, enough to mechanize a Marine infantry battalion.

LAV-25 IFV

Specifications
Weight: 14 tons
Speed: 95 kph
Gun: 25mm
Ammo: 200
Troops: 6
Armor: 25mm
In Use With: USMC

IRAQI LIGHT AFVS

Iraq has purchased armored fighting vehicles (AFVs) from a wide variety of sources over the years, and so its mechanized units often had a gypsy caravan look to them. This wide variety of light armored vehicles undoubtedly complicated the maintenance and supply problems faced by Iraq's logistical services. A few of the most important light armored vehicles are detailed below.

BMP-1 INFANTRY FIGHTING VEHICLE

The Soviet BMP (*Bronevaya Maschina Piekhota*, or Armored Vehicle, Infantry) was the world's first genuine infantry fighting vehicle (IFV), and most nations have scrambled to follow suit. The German *Marder*, British Warrior, French AMX-10P, Dutch AIFV, and American M2 Bradley all trace their origin to the appearance of the BMP in Red Square in November of 1967.

What the BMP is designed to do is combine a specialized firepower support vehicle with a traditional armored troop carrier. This allows the squad to travel under armor on the road (which makes it more difficult for artillery to disrupt the forward movement of the unit). Then when the infantry dismounts for the attack, the BMP follows and provides additional firepower as needed. In effect, it enables the squad to carry around a recoilless rifle and an ATGM launcher, plus a fair amount of ammunition for both, without burdening the riflemen in the squad.

On thing that the BMP was never intended to do was carry its rifle squad forward into the area swept by enemy direct fire; its armor is proof only against artillery fragments. The Iraqis have mounted additional armor blocks on the sides of some of their BMPs, but even this does not enable it to tackle heavy gun systems.

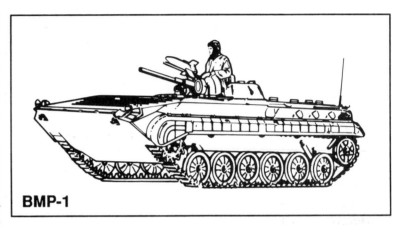

BMP-1

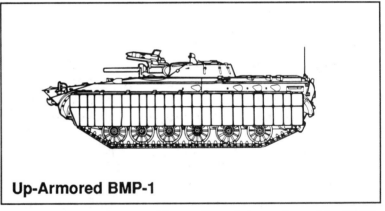

Up-Armored BMP-1

Most of Iraq's BMPs are concentrated in the mechanized brigades of the Republican Guard. A number of the BMPs in Iraqi service are actually Czech-produced BVP-1s.

Specifications

Weight: 14 tons
Road Speed: 70 kph
Gun: 73mm smoothbore
Missile: AT-3 Sagger
Passengers: 8 infantrymen
Rounds Carried: 40 cannon rounds, 5 missiles
Armor: 15-20mm (perhaps 30mm on up-armored versions)
Number on Hand: 1000

TYPE 63 ARMORED PERSONNEL CARRIER

This is the standard Chinese APC, and has been purchased by Iraq in considerable numbers. It is lightly armored, mechanically unreliable, and generally not highly thought of. It is usually used by mechanized elements of infantry divisions (such as the divisional special forces battalion) or motorized infantry divisions. The mechanized infantry that conducted the attack on Khafji used this APC.

Specifications
Weight: 12 tons
Road Speed: 65 kph
Gun: 12.7mm machinegun
Passengers: 13 infantrymen
Armor: 5-10mm
Number on Hand: 1000+

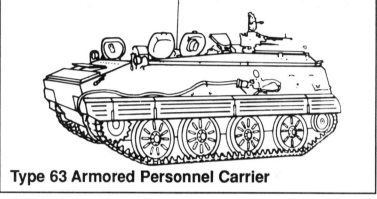

Type 63 Armored Personnel Carrier

ERC-90 ARMORED CAR

This French Panhard ERC-90 armored car has been widely exported, and is also used by the French Army. (No French units active in Desert Storm were equipped with it, however.) Its oversized turret, very long gun, and boat-shaped hull make it a distinctive vehicle. The brigade recon company of the mechanized brigade which attacked Khafji was partially equipped with these vehicles, and at least one was knocked out during the fighting there.

Specifications
Weight: 8.3 tons
Road Speed: 80 kph
Gun: 90mm
Rounds Carried: 30
Armor: 10-15mm

BTR-60 ARMORED PERSONNEL CARRIER

The four axles and lozenge-shaped hull of the BTR-60 have become a trademark of Soviet-equipped armies. This is a common APC in Iraqi service, supplemented by the similar Czech OT-64. Its similarity in general layout to the USMC LAV-25 undoubtedly contributed to the friendly fire incident during the battle for Khafji.

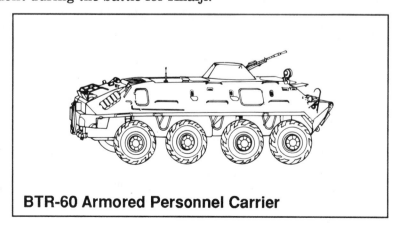

ERC-90 Armored Car

Specifications
Weight: 10 tons
Road Speed: 80 kph
Gun: 12.7mm machinegun
Passengers: 8 infantrymen
Armor: 7-9mm
Number on Hand: 1000+

BTR-60 Armored Personnel Carrier

FIRE FOR EFFECT MODERN FIELD ARTILLERY

As armies have become increasingly mechanized, artillery has lost the ability to dominate the battlefield it once had. Most mobile forces are carried in armored vehicles which are proof against artillery fragments.

A new generation of munitions is restoring artillery as an important component of the combined arms team, however. These are widely referred to as "submunition" rounds, meaning the round bursts in the air and scatters a large number of smaller munitions over a wide area. The two most common types of submunitions are ICM and FASCAM.

ICM (Improved Conventional Munitions) rounds are filled with dozens of 40mm shaped charge grenades. These are devastating to infantry or gun crews in the open, and so are ideal rounds for silencing towed artillery units. (Of Iraq's 3500 field guns, 3000 are towed instead of self-propelled.) Of equal importance, their HEAT warhead also has the ability to disable lightly armored vehicles, such as APCs and IFVs, and can even damage tanks given a lucky hit.

FASCAM (Field Artillery Scatterable Mines) rounds allow artillery units to quickly lay antitank and antipersonnel mine fields several kilometers away from the closest friendly troops—a tremendously valuable ability in mobile warfare. This gives a rapidly moving mechanized force the ability to screen its own flanks and blunt enemy counterattacks by sowing mine barriers in the path of advancing mobile reserves.

ALLIED ARTILLERY

The coalition forces employed a fairly homogeneous selection of guns and rockets. Both the United States and the United Kingdom used the US-built multiple-launch rocket system (MLRS), and the US also employed a few tactical missile systems (TACMS) on an experimental basis. These are launched from the same vehicle as the MLRS, but the launcher can only carry two TACMSs instead of 12 rockets.

The most common tube artillery used by the Coalition was the 155mm howitzer, either the M-109A2 self-propelled version or the M-198 towed version. For heavy fire missions, the 203mm (8") M-110A2 self-propelled howitzer was used.

The French employed their own GCT self-propelled and TR towed 155mm howitzers. The Egyptian divisions were mostly equipped with US-built weapons while the Saudis and other gulf states used a mixture of US and French guns.

Virtually all of these weapons could fire both conventional and submunition rounds.

COALITION ARTILLERY SYSTEMS
Towed Guns
System: M-198 155mm
Max. Range: 24 km

System: TR 155mm
Max. Range: 18 km

Self-Propelled Guns
System: M-109A2 (SP) 155mm
Max. Range: 18 km

System: M-110A2 (SP) 203mm
Max. Range: 19 km

System: GCT (SP) 155mm
Max. Range: 21 km

Multiple-Rocket Launchers
System: MLRS 227mm
Rockets: 12
Max. Range: 32 km

System: TACMS 800mm
Missiles: 2
Max. Range: 96 km

IRAQI ARTILLERY

The Iraqis began the war with a large and quite varied collection of artillery systems. They had 3000 towed guns, 500 self-propelled guns, and 200 multiple-rocket launchers. Many of these were Soviet systems of indifferent performance and limited to conventional rounds. The Iraqis held a number of very capable artillery systems of Western manufacture as well, though.

The most interesting of these was a series of 155mm guns designed by the Canadian-born ballistics expert Dr. Gerald Bull. Bull may now be best known for his alleged design of a multichamber "supergun" for Iraq, the components for which were apparently seized by British customs. The full truth behind this particular project may never emerge, as Bull was assassinated in Belgium in March of 1990. The assassins are unknown, but rumors point to Israeli intelligence.

Whether or not the supergun would have worked, Bull's conventional 155mm guns are extraordinary. Iraq owned about 100 South African-built G-5 guns and 200 Austrian-built GHN-45 guns of this design, both of which outranged any gun in the Coalition arsenal.

Also of interest were the 60 Brazilian-built Astros-II multiple-rocket launchers. These were very modern and effective systems, capable of firing a variety of ammunition types, including submunition rounds. The rocket containers are also the launchers, and are modular in design so that the launch vehicle can fire either 127mm, 180mm, or 300mm rockets. It is also interesting to note that Iraq's failure to pay for these weapons forced the Brazilian manufacturer into bankruptcy.

The main disadvantage Iraqi artillery suffered from was that it was mostly towed. Towed guns are more vulnerable than self-propelled guns, and this was a crippling liability in the face of Allied air superiority. Despite its impressive pre-war gun park, Iraqi artillery was unable to intervene effectively throughout the war, and every time it attempted to do so it was quickly smothered by Allied counterbattery fire.

IRAQI ARTILLERY SYSTEMS
Towed Guns
System: M56 105mm
Max. Range: 13 km

System: D-74 122mm
Max. Range: 24 km

System: D-30 122mm
Max. Range: 15 km

System: M1938 122mm
Max. Range: 12 km

System: M-46 130mm
Max. Range: 32 km

System: M1943 152mm
Max. Range: 12 km

System: M1937 152mm
Max. Range: 17 km

System: G-5 155mm
Max. Range: 30 km

System: GHN-45 155mm
Max. Range: 30 km

System: 2A36 152mm
Max. Range: 27 km

System: S-23 180mm
Max. Range: 30 km

Self-Propelled Guns
System: 2S1 122mm
Max. Range: 15 km

System: 2S3 152mm
Max. Range: 18 km

System: "Majnoon" 155mm
Max. Range: 30 km

System: "Al Fao" 210mm
Max. Range: 45 km

Multiple-Rocket Launchers
System: Astros II SS-30 127mm

Rockets: 32
Max. Range: 30 km

System: Astros II SS-40 180mm
Rockets: 16
Max. Range: 35 km

System: Astros II SS-60 300mm
Rockets: 4
Max. Range: 60 km

System: M-1975 122mm
Rockets: 12
Max. Range: 20 km

System: BM-21 122mm
Rockets: 40
Max. Range: 20 km

System: BM-13 132mm
Rockets: 16
Max. Range: 8 km

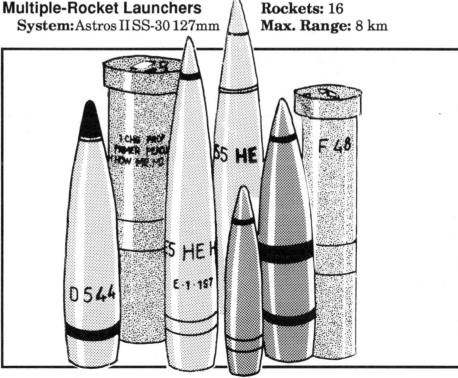

COALITION AIRCRAFT

The effective use of air power today requires the complementary use of several kinds of aircraft. These include: fighters (including antisurface-to-air missile fighters), attack, bombers, surveillance and control, reconnaissance, electronic combat, tanker, transport, and many more.

INTERCEPTORS
F-14 Tomcat

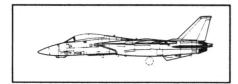

Crew: 2
Top Speed: Mach 2.4
Acceleration: Good
Maneuverability: Good
Signature: Large
Sensors: Excellent radar, zoom TV, IR tracker
Combat Radius: 500 nm (928 km)
Min. Runway: 3000 ft.
Air-to-Air Armaments: 20mm cannon, 4 missiles Phoenix, AIM-7 or AIM-9
Air-to-Ground Armaments: General-purpose bombs
Night/All-Weather Capabilities: Air-to-air, outstanding; air-to-ground, marginal
Air Refuelable?: Yes
Year Operational: 1974
In Use With: US Navy

The mission of the Tomcat is to reach out and touch antiship missiles carrying bombers before they launch. With a revolutionary fire control system and the exceptionally long-range Phoenix missile, it is very capable in that mission. The Navy also tried to combine the attributes of an interceptor and a fighter in the F-14. To a degree they succeeded. It's not a great dogfighter, but it ain't shabby either.

Tornado F-3

Crew: 2
Top Speed: 800 kts
Acceleration: Good
Maneuverability: Good
Signature: Large
Sensors: Excellent radar
Combat Radius: 750 nm (1390 km)
Min. Runway: 3000 ft.
Air-to-Air Armaments: AIM-9
Air-to-Ground Armaments: GP bombs, Sky Flash, ASM
Night/All-Weather Capabilities: Air-to-air, excellent
Year Operational: 1982
In Use With: United Kingdom

FIGHTERS
F-15C Eagle

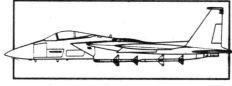

Crew: 1
Top Speed: 1342 kts (2485 kph)
Acceleration: Outstanding
Maneuverability: Excellent
Signature: Large
Sensors: Outstanding radar
Combat Radius: 645 nm
Min. Runway: 4000 ft.
Air-to-Air Armaments: 20mm cannon, 4×AIM-7, 4×AIM-9
Air-to-Ground Armaments: General-purpose bombs
Night/All-Weather Capabilities: Air-to-air, outstanding
Air Refuelable?: Yes
Year Operational: 1974
In Use With: USAF, Saudi Arabia, Israel

The F-15C Eagle is arguably the best all-around air superiority fighter in operational use today. Its exceptionally powerful and sophisticated radar makes it likely it will see its prey first.

Mirage 2000

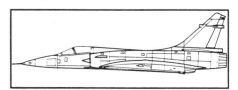

Crew: 1
Top Speed: Mach 2.2, 800 kts, 1482 kph, 921 mph
Acceleration: Excellent
Maneuverability: Outstanding
Signature: Medium
Sensors: Very good
Combat Radius: 800 nm
Min. Runway: 4000 ft.
Air-to-Air Armaments: 2×30mm gun, Matra 550 Magic, Matra Super 530
Air-to-Ground Armaments: ASM, LG, GP bombs, ARW
Night/All-Weather Capabilities: Good
Air Refuelable?: No
Year Operational: 1979
In Use With: France

The latest in the long series of Mirage delta-wing aircraft, the 2000 was designed first and foremost to be an air-superiority fighter, but was also given some attack capability.

F-4G Wild Weasel
Crew: 2

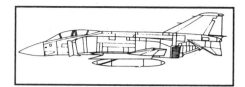

Top Speed: Mach 2.0
Acceleration: Fair
Maneuverability: Fair
Signature: Large
Sensors: Good radar, special sensors to locate electronic emissions
Combat Radius: 700 miles
Min. Runway: 8000 ft.
Air-to-Air Armaments: 2×AIM-9
Air-to-Ground Armaments: Shrike, HARM
Night/All-Weather Capabilities: Excellent
Air Refuelable?: Yes
Year Operational: F-4 1960, F-4G 1975
In Use With: USAF

The heavy losses the US Air Force suffered to North Vietnamese surface-to-air missiles and antiaircraft artillery prompted the creation of a new type of fighter—one designed not to duel with enemy fighters, but with enemy ground-based antiair weapons. The numbers and lethal power of such weapons and the effectiveness of the F-4G's special equipment and crews specially trained in the countering of that threat make the Weasels one of the most valuable weapons in an air commander's arsenal.

FIGHTER/ATTACK
F-16 Falcon

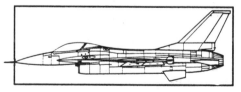

Crew: 1
Top Speed: 1400 kts, 2250 kph
Acceleration: Outstanding
Maneuverability: Outstanding
Signature: Small
Sensors: Good radar
Combat Radius: 500 nm
Min. Runway: 8000 ft.
Air-to-Air Armaments: 20mm cannon, 2×AIM-9
Air-to-Ground Armaments: GP/EO/LG bombs, CBU, Maverick missiles
Night/All-Weather Capabilities: Air-to-air, fair; air-to-ground, fair (with Mavericks only)
Air Refuelable?: Yes
Year Operational: 1979
In Use With: USAF

The F-16 made famous the concept of the "swing fighter," a craft that could fight air-to-air until air superiority was achieved and then attack enemy surface units. It represents the strengths and weaknesses of this approach. Probably the world's most maneuverable fighter, it is exceptionally capable in close-in dogfight. However, it lacks long or intermediate range missiles, so it could get shot down before ever getting close enough to show its stuff. Although it is an extremely accurate bomb dropper, some feel it flies too fast to pick out a deployed enemy and the long runway it requires makes it unlikely to be based close enough to the front to be responsive to a quickly evolving ground situation.

F/A-18 Hornet

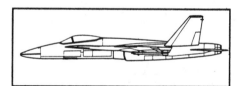

Crew: 1
Top Speed: 1.8 Mach+
Acceleration: Very good
Maneuverability: Excellent
Signature: Medium
Sensors: Very good
Combat Radius: 575 nm (1065 km)
Min. Runway: 2000 ft.
Air-to-Air Armaments: 1×20mm cannon, 2×AIM-9, 2×AIM-7
Air-to-Ground Armaments: GP/EO/LG bombs, CBU
Night/All-Weather Capabilities: Air-to-air, good; air-to-ground, good
Air Refuelable?: Yes
Year Operational: 1979
In Use With: US Navy, US Marine

Corps, Canada

This was the US Navy's choice for a "swing fighter" and embodies a different set of trade-offs. While not quite as good a dogfighter as the F-16, it does possess an intermediate-range air-to-air missile.

Mirage F-1

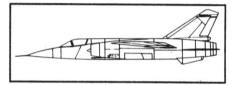

Crew: 1
Top Speed: 800 kts, 1480 kph
Acceleration: Excellent
Maneuverability: Excellent
Signature: Medium
Sensors: Good
Combat Radius: 650 nm (1200 km)
Min. Runway: 4000 ft.
Air-to-Air Armaments: 2×300 DEFA cannon, missiles
Air-to-Ground Armaments: GP/LG bombs, rockets, AGM, antiradar missiles
Night/All-Weather Capabilities: Limited
Air Refuelable?: Yes
Year Operational: 1967
In Use With: Iraq, France, Qatar

The F-1 is France's entry into the "swing fighter" field.

F-5E Tiger II

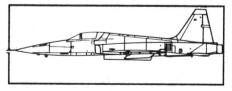

Crew: 1

Top Speed: 710 kts, 1314 kph
Acceleration: Good
Maneuverability: Good
Signature: Very small
Sensors: Poor
Combat Radius: 120 nm (222 km)
Min. Runway: 3000 ft.
Air-to-Air Armaments: 2×20mm cannon, 2×AIM-9
Air-to-Ground Armaments: GP/LG bombs, CBU, rockets, 1×30mm gun pod
Night/All-Weather Capabilities: Virtually none
Air Refuelable?: No
Year Operational: 1972
In Use With: Saudi Arabia

The original F-5A was a relatively cheap and easy to maintain aircraft the US gave to friendly Third World countries so they would think they had a jet fighter. But with the advent of lighter, cheaper, smaller electronics, the F-5 has evolved into quite a respectable and versatile combat aircraft. The F-5F's remaining weakness is its exceptionally small combat radius.

ATTACK
A-7D Corsair II

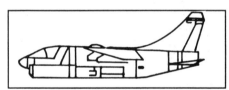

Crew: 1
Top Speed: 600 kts, 1126 kph
Acceleration: Fair
Maneuverability: Fair
Signature: Small
Sensors: Fair radar
Combat Radius: 700 nm
Min. Runway: 7000 ft.
Air-to-Air Armaments: 1×20mm cannon, 4×AIM-9
Air-to-Ground Armaments: GP/EO/LG bombs, CBU, rockets, 30mm gun pod, Maverick missile
Night/All-Weather Capabilities: Limited, principally with Maverick
Air Refuelable?: Yes
Year Operational: 1966
In Use With: US Navy

A-10 Thunderbolt II (a.k.a. Warthog)

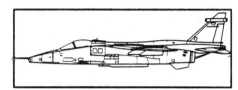

Crew: 1
Top Speed: 380 kts, 709 kph
Acceleration: Poor
Maneuverability: Good
Signature: Large
Sensors: None
Combat Radius: 250 nm
Min. Runway: 4000 ft.
Air-to-Ground Armaments: 2×AIM-9
Air-to-Ground Armaments: 1×30mm cannon, GP/EO/LG bombs, CBU/BLU
Night/All-Weather Capabilities: Limited, principally with Maverick
Air Refuelable?: Yes
Year Operational: 1972
In Use With: USAF

AV-8B Harrier

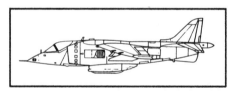

Crew: 1
Top Speed: 650 kts, 1176 kph
Acceleration: Fair
Maneuverability: Good
Signature: Small
Sensors: None
Combat Radius: 260 nm (418 km)
Min. Runway: 0
Air-to-Air Armaments: 2×30mm cannon, 2×AIM-9 missiles
Air-to-Ground Armaments: 5000 lbs. total bomb load; GP bombs, rockets
Night/All-Weather Capabilities: Limited
Air Refuelable?: No
Year Operational: 1982
In Use With: US Marine Corps

The Harrier is the first successful vertical takeoff and landing combat aircraft, though a short takeoff role is needed for normal range and weapons load. While the Harrier's range and weapons load is not impressive, its tremendous basing flexibility allows it to operate very close to the front lines, permitting unequaled responsiveness and sortie rates.

Jaguar

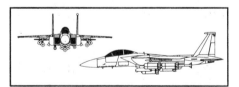

Crew: 1 or 2
Top Speed: 917 kts, 1699 kph
Acceleration: Good
Maneuverability: Good
Signature: Small
Sensors: None
Combat Radius: 495 nm (1917 km)
Min. Runway: 4000 ft.
Air-to-Air Armaments: 2×30mm cannons
Air-to-Ground Armaments: 10,500 lbs. total bomb load; GP/LG bombs, rockets, CBU/BLU
Night/All Weather Capabilities: Limited
Air Refuelable?: Yes
Year Operational: 1969
In Use With: United Kingdom, France, Oman

Developed by the United Kingdom and France as a light daytime attack aircraft; improvements have given the Jaguar a fair all-weather capability. Jaguars have to be adapted to recce and weasel use.

BOMBERS
F-15E Strike Eagle

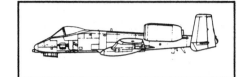

Crew: 2
Top Speed: Mach 2.5
Acceleration: Good
Maneuverability: Good
Signature: Large
Sensors: Outstanding

Combat Radius: 650
Min. Runway: 6000 ft.
Air-to-Air Armaments: 20mm gun, 4×AIM-7, 4×AIM-9
Air-to-Ground Armaments: 24,500 lbs. total bomb load
Night/All-Weather Capabilities: Outstanding
Air Refuelable?: Yes
Year Operational: 1988
In Use With: USAF

To the casual observer, it might not be possible to tell the F-15C from the F-15E. Most similarities are skin deep. The Strike Eagle is probably the most effective all-weather medium bomber flying today.

Tornado GR1

Crew: 2
Top Speed: 800 kts, 1480 kph
Acceleration: Good
Maneuverability: Good
Signature: Large
Sensors: Excellent radar
Combat Radius: 750 nm (1390 km)
Min. Runway: 3000 ft.
Air-to-Air Armaments: 2×27mm cannons, AIM-9
Air-to-Ground Armaments: LG and GP bombs, AGM, CBU/BLU, Rockets, JP233
Night/All-Weather Capabilities: Excellent
Air Refuelable?: Yes
Year Operational: 1980
In Use With: UK, Saudi Arabia, Italy

The Tornado was developed and built as a joint venture of the United Kingdom, Germany, and Italy. Both a bomber and an interceptor version were developed. This version was designed primarily as a bomber. Its primary target is enemy airfields.

F-111 Aardvark
Crew: 2

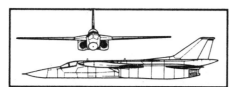

Top Speed: 1433 kts, 2655 kph
Acceleration: Fair
Maneuverability: Poor
Signature: Large
Sensors: Very good
Combat Radius: 855 nm (1800 km)
Min. Runway: 9000 ft.
Air-to-Air Armaments: 2×AIM-9
Air-to-Ground Armaments: 20,000 lbs. total bomb load; GP/EO/LG bombs, CBU
Night/All Weather Capabilities: Outstanding
Air Refuelable?: Yes
Year Operational: 1966
In Use With: USAF

The F-111 is what was salvaged from an exceptionally expensive attempt to save money by designing one aircraft to do a host of missions. After spending a lot of time and money the USAF actually managed to make the F-111 a quite effective medium bomber. (The name Aardvark is not officially sanctioned.)

A-6E Intruder

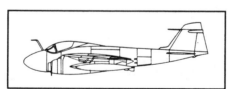

Crew: 2
Top Speed: 560 kts, 1037 kph
Acceleration: Fair
Maneuverability: Poor
Signature: Large
Sensors: Good
Combat Radius: 2,818 nm (5222 km)
Min. Runway: 5000 ft.
Air-to-Air Armaments: 2×AIM-9 missiles
Air-to-Ground Armaments: 15,000 lbs. total bomb load; GP/EO/LG bombs, CBU/BLU
Night/All-Weather Capabilities: Very good

Air Refuelable?: Yes
Year Operational: 1961
In Use With: US Navy

The venerable A-6E is the heavy hitter of carrier aviation. For most of the Vietnam War, a handful of A-6s was the United States' only true all-weather bomber in an area known for truly horrendous flying weather. Although its once impressive bomb accuracy has paled in comparison to the latest systems, it still is a very valuable member of any air team.

B-52G

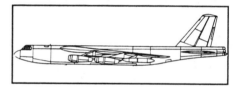

Crew: 6
Top Speed: 365 kts, 676 kph
Acceleration: Fair
Maneuverability: Poor
Signature: Huge
Sensors: Excellent
Combat Radius: 4342 nm (16,095 km)
Min. Runway: 10,000 ft.
Air-to-Air Armaments: 4×50 caliber tail gun
Air-to-Ground Armaments: 38,250 lbs. total bomb load; GP bombs, Harpoon missiles
Night/All-Weather Capabilities: Very good
Air Refuelable?: Yes
Year Operational: 1955, G model–1959
In Use With: USAF

Less than half the members of the United States Air Force were born when the B-52 first flew.

IRAQI AIRCRAFT

The Iraqi Air Force, like the Iraqi Army, had lots of equipment—a fraction of which was at or near state of the art. Given the advantage the Coalition enjoyed in numbers and quality, eventual air supremacy was almost inevitable, yet the Iraqis were potentially more of a threat than the air campaign seems to indicate. If surprise had not been achieved, or if the planning and execution of the air campaign had not been as flawless, the following aircraft could have given the Coalition trouble—at least for a while.

INTERCEPTOR
MiG-25 Foxbat/Recon

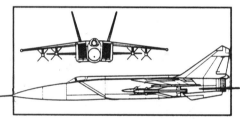

Crew: 1
Top Speed: Mach 2.83
Acceleration: Good
Maneuverability: Poor
Signature: Large
Sensors: Good
Combat Radius: 780 nm
Min. Runway: 5000 ft.
Air-to-Air Armaments: 4 air-to-air missiles
Air-to-Ground Armaments: None
Night/All-Weather Capabilities: Good
Air Refuelable?: No
Year Operational: 1966

The MiG-25 was designed the to intercept high-flying, fast-moving bombers. The Soviets have converted many of their MiG 25s to reconnaissance craft. It would be plausible to assume MiG 25s in Iraqi service are also used exclusively or primarily for reconnaissance.

FIGHTER
MiG 29 Fulcrum

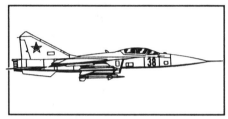

Crew: 1
Top Speed: 1260 kts, 2334 kph
Acceleration: Outstanding
Maneuverability: Outstanding
Signature: Medium
Sensors: Excellent radar, infrared sensor, and laser range finder
Combat Radius: 432 nm (800 km)
Min. Runway: 1200 ft.
Air-to-Air Armaments: 1×30mm cannon, 6×radar missiles, 6×IR missiles
Air-to-Ground Armaments: None
Night/All-Weather Capabilities: Excellent
Air Refuelable?: No
Year Operational: 1985

The Fulcrum is roughly equivalent to the F/A-18 in its overall air-to-air combat potential. It has a few features that are superior to the best Western fighters. It can also stalk its prey with its radar off, using its infrared sensor. As most combat aircraft now have devices to warn pilots when an enemy radar is "painting" their aircraft, the infrared sensor will preserve the element of surprise.

MiG-23/27 Flogger

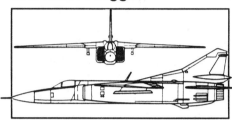

Crew: 1
Top Speed: Mach 2.3
Acceleration: Good
Maneuverability: Good
Signature: Average
Sensors: Good
Combat Radius: 650 nm
Min. Runway: 3000 ft.
Air-to-Air Armaments: 2×23mm cannon, 4×AA-8, 4×AA-7
Air-to-Ground Armaments: GP bombs, CBU
Night/All-Weather Capabilities: Fair to good, air-to-air
Air Refuelable?: No
Year Operational: 1968

The Flogger was designed as a fighter, but was also given some ability to drop bombs. Fairly competitive with Western fighters when it first became operational, the Flogger has been outclassed by newer fighters for almost 20 years.

MiG-21

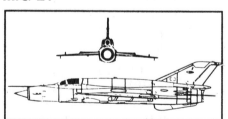

Crew: 1
Top Speed: Mach 2.05
Acceleration: Good
Maneuverability: Good

Signature: Small
Sensors: Fair
Combat Radius: 200
Min. Runway: 3000 ft.
Air-to-Air Armaments: 1×23mm gun, 2×AA-2/2D, 2×AA-20
Air-to-Ground Armaments: 3300 lbs. total bomb load; BP bombs
Night/All-Weather Capabilities: None
Air Refuelable?: No
Year Operational: 1968

In the skies over North Vietnam, the MiG-21 could be *very* competitive against the best the US had at the time. That was 20 years ago. Now, any engagements with it would not have been a contest.

The F-7 is a Chinese copy of a Soviet MiG-21 airframe using off-the-shelf Western avionics. It is produced for export.

FIGHTER/ATTACK
Su-25 Frogfoot

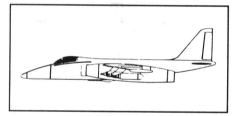

Crew: 1
Top Speed: 0.8 Mach
Acceleration: Poor
Maneuverability: Fair
Signature: Large
Sensors: Poor
Combat Radius: 300 nm
Min. Runway: 4000 ft.
Air-to-Air Armaments: 2×30mm gun, 2×AA-2D or 2×AA-8
Air-to-Ground Armaments: 9700 lbs. total bomb load; GP, LG, CBU, rockets
Night/All-Weather Capabilities: None
Air refuelable: No
Year Operational: 1982-84

The Frogfoot is sometimes called the Soviet A-10. That is being charitable

because the aircraft falls short of the A-10 in every attribute. Still, both were designed from the ground up to fight in close coordination with friendly ground forces.

Su-20 Fitter

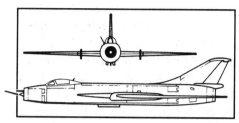

Crew: 1
Top Speed: Mach 2.09
Acceleration: Good
Maneuverability: Good
Signature: Average
Sensors: Fair
Combat Radius: 200
Min. Runway: 2000 ft.
Air-to-Air Armaments: 30×30mm gun, 1×radar, 1×IR or 2×IR
Air-to-Ground Armaments: 6617 lbs. total bomb load; GP bombs, rockets
Night/All-Weather Capabilities: None
Air Refuelable?: No
Year Operational: 1967

The Su-20 is the export version of the Su-17, the most common Soviet attack aircraft. Though not impressive, it could have done some damage.

Su-7
The predecessor of the Su-17. Less than half as capable.

F-6
The F-6 is a Chinese copy of a Soviet MiG-19 airframe using off-the-shelf Western avionics. It is produced for export. Like the F-7 the price appears to be a bargain.

BOMBERS
Su-24 Fencer
Crew: 2
Top Speed: Mach 2.8
Acceleration: Good

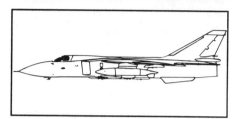

Maneuverability: Good
Signature: Large
Sensors: Excellent
Combat Radius: 970 nm
Min. Runway: 3000 ft.
Air-to-Air Armaments: Cannon
Air-to-Ground Armaments: 17,635 lbs. total bomb load; GP, LG bombs, AGM
Night/All-Weather Capabilities: Excellent
Air Refuelable?: No
Year Operational: 1974

One successful Fencer mission would have delivered more ordnance than 50 Scud strikes. However, Iraq had just received the Fencer.

Mirage F-1
(Described under Coalition Aircraft.) Excellent crews can make a weapon more formidable than the cold characteristics suggest. Iraq's F-1 pilots had received excellent French training. During the Iran-Iraq War they displayed skill, creativity, and daring during many raids deep inside Iran.

I1-28, Tu-22, Tu-16
These big bombers do carry a lot of bombs, but alone they would have been easy pickings for the air defenses of any of the gulf states.

MUNITIONS MAKE THE MISSION
COALITION AIR MUNITIONS

One of the sources of the effectiveness of air power is its flexibility and versatility. Munitions is a big part of how air power does it. Munitions allow aircraft to adapt to the target. So the key to understanding munitions is understanding targets.

Targets have three general attributes: hardness, need for precision, and danger.

Hardness: Different targets require different amounts of explosive force to destroy. There is no advantage in making the rubble bounce. Aircraft can carry only so much weight. The smaller the bomb you carry that will do the job, the more jobs you can do in one sortie.

Need for Precision: Contrary to the impression of many people after watching US, British, and French mission films, not all targets require pinpoint accuracy. For example, a bomb landing anywhere in a fuel dump will blow up the fuel dump. If you drop a dozen dumb bombs, at least one will surely hit the dump. However, sometimes the need for precision does not come from the target itself, but from the company it keeps. If the fuel dump is next door to a mosque you better hit the dump and only the dump.

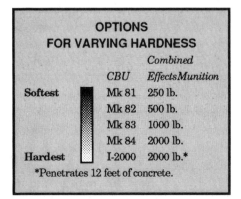

OPTIONS FOR VARYING HARDNESS

	CBU	Combined Effects Munition
Softest	Mk 81	250 lb.
	Mk 82	500 lb.
	Mk 83	1000 lb.
	Mk 84	2000 lb.
Hardest	I-2000	2000 lb.*

*Penetrates 12 feet of concrete.

Danger: If a target is important enough for you to want to destroy, it's probably important enough for the enemy to try to defend. Weapons that let you "stand off" from the target (and the target's defenses) can improve your life expectancy and, not unimportantly, improve your aim.

OPTIONS
FOR VARYING HARDNESS

The human body is very soft. Even the smallest traditional bomb would blow one soldier to smithereens but not touch a second soldier laying prone of in a foxhole just yards away. To solve this problem, the cluster bomb unit (CBU) was deployed. CBU's spread many small bomblets over a selectable area. For the same weight, many more "targets" can be rendered ineffective. Against slightly harder targets, like light armored vehicles, the combined effects munition-type CBU can be used. This type of CBU contains anti-personnel, antiarmor, and incendiary bomblets. For still harder targets the "Mk" series bombs are used. Finally, for the harder targets (like supposedly impenetrable aircraft shelters) the Improved 2000-lb. warheads (I-2000) are used.

NEED FOR PRECISION

Again, precision is not always

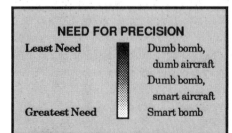

NEED FOR PRECISION

Least Need	Dumb bomb, dumb aircraft
	Dumb bomb, smart aircraft
Greatest Need	Smart bomb

needed. A harassment raid to keep and enemy awake at night really does not need to hit anything. Any aircraft with any bomb will do. Some aircraft like the F-16 can get "near" smart-bomb accuracy using conventional munitions. Most ammo dumps don't care where they are hit. However, sometimes great accuracy is called for—for example, if that ammo dump was an ammo bunker and only the door was "soft" enough for our bomb to penetrate.

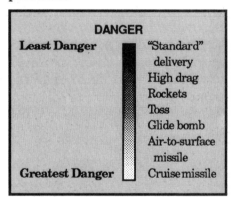

DANGER

Least Danger	"Standard" delivery
	High drag
	Rockets
	Toss
	Glide bomb
	Air-to-surface missile
Greatest Danger	Cruise missile

DANGER

When little danger is perceived (or no options are available), the pilot flies level or in a shallow dive toward the target and releases the bomb at such a distance that its momentum leaving the aircraft will carry it to the target by the time it reaches the ground. If there is small arms fire around the target, you can release a little higher—but too high, and you will probably miss the target.

Or you can go in very low. Flying "in the dirt" avoids many types of SAMs and doesn't give gunners much time to aim. However, if you dropped standard bombs that low, they would hit the ground so soon after release that your aircraft would be in the blast radius. To avoid this, the Mk series bombs can be fitted with high drag fins that will slow the bombs down enough for you not to blow yourself up.

To get farther out from the target, some sort of smart bomb is needed. A smart bomb lets you release the weapon higher or toss it farther and still hit the target. If getting close enough to let the smart bomb glide into the target is still too close, then the smart bomb can be equipped with a rocket mortar to extend the range further. If even that is too close, then this target probably requires a cruise missile.

PUTTING IT ALL TOGETHER

As an example, let's go back to that ammo bunker. Even the door is pretty hard, so you will need a Mk 83. To hit a door you will definitely need a smart bomb, so the kit that's needed to turn the Mk 83 into a smart bomb is installed. Letting the smart bomb glide in will put you out of effective range of all defenses, so no rocket mortar is needed.

OTHER SMART WEAPONS

Other air weapons have the basic characteristics of smart bombs, although they are not thought of as such.

Most air-to-air missiles use one of two types of seeker heads.

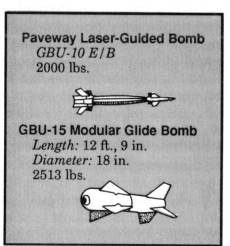

Paveway Laser-Guided Bomb
GBU-10 E/B
2000 lbs.

GBU-15 Modular Glide Bomb
Length: 12 ft., 9 in.
Diameter: 18 in.
2513 lbs.

The AIM-7 "sees" reflected radar energy and steers the missile toward it.

The AIM-9 "sees" heat, hopefully from an enemy aircraft and again guides the missile toward the heat.

The missiles used by weasel anti-SAM aircraft "see" energy from selected radar frequencies (hopefully the enemy's) and guide themselves toward it. Radars usually can tell when a antiradiation missile is heading their way and shut down. While that is good, it is even better to shut the radar down permanently. Newer missiles go faster to give the operators less time to turn off, remember where the radiation was, or both.

SPECIALIZED MUNITIONS

There are too many to name them all, but here are arguably the two most important.

Air-Scatterable Mines: If a road you want to interdict crosses a river, no problem—drop the bridge and the route is closed. But let's say your route is across the Iraqi desert. If you blow a hole in the road your enemy will simply drive around the hole. Air-scatterable mines can deny the enemy large areas and mess up his routes. They are even kind of smart; if there is no enemy to stop, they will wait for him.

Antirunway Munitions: Runways are terrible targets. To be strong enough to support the weight of aircraft, they are naturally built "hard." Yet, to stop flight operations, craters must be put in a big chunk of the runway. This has led to several specialized munitions that are just big enough for the hardness of the runway and small enough so many can be dropped. And as enemy engineers have this annoying habit of fixing runways, many antirunway munitions include antipersonnel (engineers) and anti-vehicle (bulldozer) mines.

HOW SMART BOMBS WORK

All smart bombs have the same basic components: the seeker head that "sees" if the bomb is on the path to its target, the brain of the bomb, control surfaces to make any course corrections deemed necessary, and, of course, the warhead. The seeker head may see the reflected energy of a laser or compare a visual light or infrared picture against what it was told it should see.

Early smart bombs could have been more appropriately called "fairly stupid" bombs. If the seeker head was too low, it would slam the control surfaces all the way to bring the nose of the bomb up. Of course, this would make the nose too high so it would slam the control surfaces all the way to bring the nose down. This would produce an inefficient wiggling flight path and cause many early smart bombs to fall short of their targets. Newer smarter bombs make proportional corrections and are not only more accurate, but can be released farther from their target.

That is basically how a cruise missile works. At several points along its path it compares what it sees in a radar picture to what it was told to expect and makes proportional changes to stay on course.

IRAQI GROUND-BASED AIR DEFENSE

While much attention was paid to the Iraqi Air Force (IAF), the Coalition did succeed in preventing the IAF from shooting down a single Coalition plane or bombing a single Coalition target. On the other hand, little has been reported on Iraqi ground-based air defenses, yet they were responsible for all 56 Coalition aircraft that were lost due to hostile action. What were these defenses, and why were Iraq's relatively cheap ground-based air defenses so much more effective than its air force?

Iraq spent considerable time and money building up an integrated air defense system. The system had four basic components: radars, a command and control network to direct the battle, ground-based air defenses at key locations, and fighters standing by for air defense missions (as a kind of strategic reserve).

In the first seconds of Desert Storm, Coalition air forces went a long way toward *dis*integrating this integrated system. The radars were among the first targets, and the command and control network (from the headquarters of the IAF to hardened air defense sector control centers) was also hard hit that first night. US Air Force F-4G Wild Weasels and US Navy A-7Es

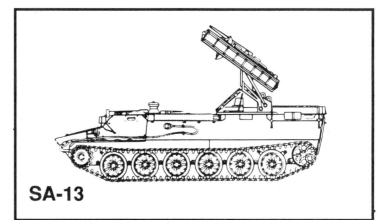

SA-13

were out in force, shutting down all the SAM sites they could. Royal Air Force Tornados flew in the teeth of formidable air base defenses, and closed the Iraqi Air Force down, but paid a price, suffering the highest proportional losses of any aircraft in the Coalition.

After a week, all the Iraqis had left of their integrated air defense system were the ground-based systems. Intelligence assets quickly located the large radars and command centers and it is difficult for a runway to hide from a satellite that can allegedly read a license plate from orbit. All of these targets were relatively easy to find and to destroy.

Ground-based air defense systems are tougher to destroy. There are a lot more of them than airfields and command bunkers. They are easier to hide from aerial and satellite reconnaissance, and they can move much more readily once discovered. Their individual effectiveness was very much reduced by the destruction of their radars and the command and control network, but individual components could and did remain a danger until neutralized.

SURFACE-TO-AIR MISSILES (SAMS)
SA-2 Guideline
Range: 31 miles
Altitude: High

The US had pretty much figured out how to defeat this 1950s vintage missile by the end of the Vietnam War. Moving an SA-2 launch site takes considerable time and effort.

SA-3 Goa
Range: 18 miles
Altitude: Medium

The Goa is almost as old as the SA-2, but it is considerably more mobile.

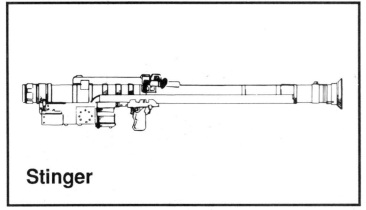

Stinger

SA-6 Gainful

Range: 37 miles
Altitude: Medium

Although the Gainful was first spotted in 1967, it did not receive its world reputation until the 1973 Arab-Israeli War, where it took a terrible toll in Israeli aircraft despite how low they flew (a technique used to defeat earlier, more primitive SAMs).

SA-7 Grail

Range: 6 miles
Altitude: Low

The SA-7 is reported to be a copy of the first US shoulder-fired SAM (the FIM 43A Redeye, now obsolete). The SA-7 is an early heat-seeker, and is only effective when fired at a target moving away from the launcher. It is highly mobile and can be set up quickly.

SA-13 Gropher

Range: 5 miles
Altitude: Low to medium

The Gropher appeared in the mid-1970s. It is a heat-seeking missile mounted on a tracked vehicle. It is teamed with the ZSU-23-4 to provide air defense to the armored units of the Republican Guard.

I-Hawk

Range: 25 miles
Altitude: All

Kuwait had four batteries of I-Hawk (Improved-Hawk) surface-to-air missiles which were captured by the Iraqis during the invasion. The I-Hawk is an extremely effective system, but there is no evidence that they were ever used. Either the Iraqis were unable to learn to use them in time or the I-Hawk sites were among the first Coalition targets.

FIM-92A Stinger

Range: 11 miles

Altitude: Low

Kuwait is known to have had a number of FIM-92A Stingers. It is not known whether any of these were used against Coalition aircraft.

ANTIAIRCRAFT ARTILLERY (AAA)

Antiaircraft artillery (AAA) works on the principle of numbers. The smaller guns work by throwing great numbers of rounds in the path of a target. The bigger guns use a large shell with a bursting charge to scatter a great number of fragments in the path of a target. Some guns rely on the gunner to locate the target visually and lead it (like a hunter leads a duck) so that the shells and the target arrive in approximately the same place in the sky at the same time. Others are linked to a radar that points the gun in the proper

direction—these are vulnerable to attack by antiradar missiles.

Aircraft have several ways to counter the effects of AAA fire. They can fly higher than the shells can reach. They can suppress or destroy the AAA guns' targeting radar. They can interfere with command and communications channels. They can fly in conditions when the gunners cannot see well. They can use "smart" weapons to attack from beyond the AAA guns' range.

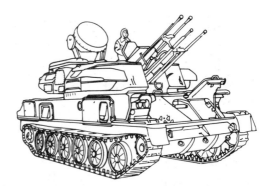

ZSU-23-4

ANTIAIRCRAFT ARTILLERY

Type	Caliber	Notes
ZPU 1/2/4	14.5mm	Short range
ZU-23	23mm	
M1939	37mm	
S-60	57mm	Fixed sites
KS-12	85mm	
KS-19	100mm	
KS-30	130mm	Long range
ZSU-23-4	23mm	Range: 1 mile, mobile, quadruple barreled
ZSU-57-2	57mm	Range: 2 miles, double barreled

COALITION AIR FORCES

It would be totally untrue to say the Coalition won the war solely through air power. Still, as the picture emerges from interviews with Iraqi prisoners of war it would appear air power can claim a greater share of the credit then in any war to date. Yet, six months before the opening of Desert Storm, this great air armada did not exist as a single force. How did the many air forces of the Coalition come together and build a force capable, against a worthy foe, of gaining air superiority in hours, air supremacy in days and ground and naval forces victory in weeks?

THE LONG VIEW

The United States Air Force supplied the air component commander for the Coalition air force and a majority of the aircraft. Understanding the US Air Force is a good start in understanding the Coalition's air power.

Many of the origins of the Coalition's victory in the skies over Iraqi can be traced to America's defeat in Vietnam. The now famous smart bombs had their genesis in US Air Force's frustration in not being able to knock out North Vietnamese bridges. North Vietnam's formidable air defenses gave rise to:

- Specialized SAM-hunting fighters (the F-4G Wild Weasel)
- Airborne surveillance and control aircraft (the E-3 Sentry Airborne Warning and Control System (AWACS))
- Force package tactics
- A dedicated air-to-air combat aircraft with a gun (the F-15 Eagle)
- Schools not in how to fly, but how to fight (the US Navy's Top Gun, the US Air Force's Fighter School and Red Flag exercises)

FROM MANY, MANY

It at first seems remarkable that the air forces of so many nations could plan and execute a single cohesive air campaign. There are several factors that contributed to this success:

- About half the Coalition's non-US air power came from nations that are members of NATO. These airmen had been planning and exercising with American airmen for over 40 years.
- The other half of the Coalition's non-US air power was contributed by the members of the Gulf Cooperation Council. They had considerable experience working together and varying levels of experience working with the US Air Force.
- English is the universal language of aviation, so communication was not a significant problem.
- US Air Force doctrine calls for centralized direction but decentralized execution. There was one plan but each air force could fly its missions the way its own equipment, training, and doctrine dictated.

TWO POUNDS INTO A ONE-POUND BAG

When US soldiers who fought in Vietnam meet, invariably one of the first questions asked is, "Where were you when?" At different points in that long war various parts of South Vietnam were relatively safe or very "hot." Coalition Air Force members who meet years from now will ask, "Where you were based?" for a slightly different reason.

The US and many of its NATO allies sent so many aircraft to the gulf that every base, regardless of type, was used to maximum capacity. Aside from the range of accommmodations, the basing squeeze had serious military implications. At the main air bases, the aircraft shelters were second to none, but at the commercial airports and bare bases aircraft were at first parked side by side without protection. Finally, there just wasn't any more space. The B-52s could have moved closer, but there just was no space to park them. So they flew from Diego Garcia (an island in the middle of the Indian Ocean) and from England. The long trip meant fewer sorties could be flown.

The US Navy helped by bringing their runways with them—six aircraft carrier task forces. However, the geography worked against the navy. The gulf is a small, shallow body of water *not* conducive to carrier operations. The carriers could seldom get enough wind over their decks to permit their aircraft to take off with full fuel or bomb loads. If the carriers stayed in more open

ORDER OF BATTLE

United States Air Force

Aircraft	Number	Type	Units
F-15C	144	Fighter	1, 33, 36 TFW
F-4G	48	Wld Weasel	35, 52 TFW
F-16	288	Ftr/Attack	50,363,388,401 TFW
A-10	192	Attack	10, 23, 354 TFW
F-117A	44	Bomber	37 TFW
F-15E	72	Bomber	4 TFW
F-111F	36	Bomber	48 TFW
B-52	80?	Bomber	
TR-1A	6	Recon	17 RW
RF-4	48	Recon	117 TRW
RC-135	?	Recon	
E-3	5	Srvlnce & Ctrl	552 AWCW
E-8	2	Srvlnce & Ctrl	
OA-10	24	Srvlnce & Ctrl	23 TACS
EF-111	12	Elctrnic Cmbt	366 TFW
EC-135	?	Elctrnic Cmbt	
KC-135, KC-10	162	Aerial Refuel	
C-130	288	Tact. Airlift	

US Navy

Six of the US Navy's 12 operational aircraft carrier battle groups fought in Desert Storm. They were:

In the Red Sea	In the Gulf
USS *America*	USS *Ranger*
USS *Saratoga*	USS *Midway*
USS *Kennedy*	USS *Roosevelt*

The composition of carrier air wings may vary. The following figures are approximate (antisubmarine aircraft not listed).:

Aircraft	Number	Type
F-14	144	Fighter/Interceptor
F-18	120	Fighter/Attack
A-7	24	Fighter/Attack
A-6E	60	Bomber
E-2C	24	Surveillance & Control
EA-6B	24	Electronic Combat
KA-6D	24	Tanker

US Marine Corps

Based on the number of marine ground units that participated in Desert Storm, the following are plausible numbers for participating marine aircraft.

Aircraft	Number	Type
F/A-18	120	Fighter/Attack
(Some may be embarked on carriers)		
AV-8B	168	Attack
OV-10	30	Surveillance & Control

Saudi Arabia

Aircraft	Number	Type
F-15	57	Fighter
(May have received 12 more before Desert Storm; Saudi F-15s have some ground attack capability.)		
Tornado F3	2	Fighter
(All may not have been delivered.)		
F-5E	70	Fighter/Attack
Tornado GR1	48	Bomber
(All may not have been delivered.)		
RF-5E	10	Reconnaissance
E-3A	4	Survlance & Cntrl
KE-3A	?	Tanker
KC-135	6	Tanker
KC-130H	8	Tanker
C-130	35	Transports
Various other types	50	Transports

United Kingdom

Aircraft	Number	Type
Tornado F3	18	Interceptor/Fighter
Jaguar GR1	12	Attack
Tornado GR1	63	Bomber
Buccaneer	4	Bomber
VC-10K	?	Tanker

France

Aircraft	Number	Type
Mirage 2000	12	Fighter
F/A-18	24	Fighter/Attack

Canada

Aircraft	Number	Type
F/A-18	24	Fighter/Attack

Italy

Aircraft	Number	Type
Tornado GR1	10	Bomber

Kuwait

(Many KAF aircraft were destroyed in August.)

Aircraft	Number	Type
Mirage F-1CK	32	Fighter/Interceptor
A-4KU	30	Attack

Bahrain

Aircraft	Number	Type
F-5E/F	12	Fighter/Attack

Qatar

Aircraft	Number	Type
Mirage F-1	12	Fighter/Attack
Hunter	2	Fighter/Attack
AlphaJet	6	AlphaJet

United Arab Emirates (UAE)

Aircraft	Number	Type
Mirage 5	29	Interceptor
AlphaJet	3	Attack
C-130	5	Transport
Many types	23	Transport

Oman

Aircraft	Number	Type
Jaguar	20	Attack
Hunter	12	Attack
C-130	3	Transport
Other	26	Transport

South Korea

Aircraft	Number	Type
C-130	5	Transport

Turkey

Aircraft of the Turkish Air Force and combat aircraft sent from several NATO nations to Turkey are not included because, while ready to respond to an attack on Turkey, they did not take part in Operation Desert Storm.

waters, Iraq and Kuwait would be at the extreme range of their aircraft.

Fortunately the US Navy remembered a trick both they and the Japanese Navy used during World War II. Aircraft would take off from the carrier and land at a land strip to take on more fuel and munitions. After perhaps several sorties, the aircraft would return to the carrier. The forward strip needed little ramp and no revetments because the aircraft were only on the ground for short periods of time. Also, few support troops were needed, as most maintenance was done back on the carrier.

ANALYSIS

The combination of the F-15 and the E-3 gave the Coalition air forces the best air defense in the world. The Royal Air Force Tornados are arguably the best runway busters in the world.

The small number of F-117As gave the Coalition a capability for strategic offensive unmatched before in warfare.

The with help the E-8 Joint Stars and forward air controllers, A-10 tank killers and Apache helicopters could devastate ground forces.

The only Achilles heel of the Coalition air forces was the overcrowding of many airfields. If a lucky aircraft or Scud got through, the death toll could have been high. Little wonder shutting down Iraq's air and missile forces were a high Coalition priority.

THE COALITION FLEETS
SEA POWER

Among the first forces available to respond to the crisis in the Persian Gulf were the elements of the US Navy on station in and near the Indian Ocean. These vessels were used to support early landings of marines in Saudi Arabia and to enforce the embargo against Iraq. A number of Allied nations quickly dispatched warships to the area to assist in enforcing the blockade.

As naval strength in the region has grown, increasing attention has been paid to the manner in which naval forces can assist conventional ground operations. Control of the sea lanes is a critical mission, especially when the Allied forces are operation at the end of a long seaborne supply route. Given the relative balance of naval forces in the gulf, however, the Allied navies seem completely capable of meeting that challenge.

Beyond sea control, the navies can exert a direct effect on the land and air battle by three means: air power, naval gunfire, and missile fire.

NAVAL GUNFIRE

Naval gunfire is the traditional means used by navies to support land forces. Most modern ships, however, rely primarily on sophisticated missile systems to engage enemy ships, which are generally too expensive to use to pound ground forces.

The United States, however, maintains several big *Iowa*-class battleships, refurbished to carry naval cruise missiles but still mounting nine 16" guns for shore bombardment. These weapons would be ideal for supporting ground actions almost anywhere in Kuwait.

NAVAL MISSILES

A second means is by long-range missile fire. Although many naval warheads are too small to be worth the money to fire at ground targets, this is not true of the Tomahawk. These long-range missiles have a large warhead and are capable of pinpoint accuracy. Many US naval vessels, including the two battleships in the area, are capable of carrying them, and many vessels deployed to the region carried a much higher number than normal.

The powerful aegis cruisers that form the core of any carrier battle group's escort are highly capable air defense cruisers with very sophisticated radars. The overwhelming air superiority enjoyed by the Allies in the gulf, however, brought into question how useful their large SAM armament would be. As a result, most of them appear to have left with twice their normal Tomahawk load, at the expense of SAMs. Aegis cruisers with vertical launch capability (the more modern ships) normally carry 12 Tomahawks and 110 Standard SAMs. Most of those deployed to the gulf had between 24 and 48 Tomahawks per ship, while the *San Jacinto* was redesignated a "special weapons platform" and carried about 100 Tomahawks. In addition, there were usually between six and eight US nuclear submarines in the region with up to 100 Tomahawks between them.

In all, there were probably between 300 and 500 Tomahawk land-attack cruise missiles on naval vessels around Iraq. This tremendous concentration of cruise missiles provided the navy with the ability to make a large number of precision strikes on strategic Iraqi targets early on in the air war, such as airfields, munitions facilities, and command control complexes.

NAVAL AIR POWER

Each US attack carrier has an air group of about 74 planes, which usually includes:

24 F-14A Tomcat (fighter)
24 F/A-18 Hornet (fighter/attack)
10 A-6E Intruder (long-range attack)
8 S-3 Viking (antisubmarine)
4 EA-6B Prowler (electronic warfare)
4 E-2C Hawkeye (airborne early warning)

The Tomcat is one of the most sophisticated and effective air superiority aircraft in the world.

The Hornet can be used as either an attack aircraft or a very agile fighter. Normally it flies attack missions while the Tomcats fly top cover.

Intruders are long-range fighter-bombers. Special conformal, high-capacity fuel tanks are available to turn up to four of the ship Intruders into tankers as well, allowing the combat air patrol (CAP) to stay airborne longer, or giving strike missions a longer reach.

Vikings are ASW platforms of little use in the gulf. However, they are also strike aircraft and carry bombs.

Prowlers use electronic systems to locate and jam enemy air defense radars.

Hawkeyes use their powerful long-range radar to track any incoming aircraft, alert the carrier, and direct fighters to the intruders. Half a dozen Hawkeyes gave the Israeli Air Force a decisive edge over the Syrians in Lebanon. US carriers will deploy over 20 of them.

Carrier aircraft bring their airfields with them. Deployment of Allied aircraft to Saudi Arabia and the gulf states has filled every usable airfield to capacity, and additional air reinforcement virtually had to be by means of carriers. Also, it is much more difficult to hit a carrier than a land base because of its mobility.

NAVAL ORDER OF BATTLE
United States Navy
Persian Gulf Squadron
Command Ships: *LaSalle, Blue Ridge*
Battleships (BBG): *Missouri* (TH), *Wisconsin* (TH)
Missile Cruisers: *England* (TH), *Horne* (TH)
Destroyer: *David Ray* (TH)
Frigates: *Bradley, Reid, Barbey, Vandergrift, Taylor, Rentz, Jarrett*
Minesweepers: *Adroit, Leader, Avenger, Impervious*

Persian Gulf Amphibious Group
Helicopter Carrier: *Inchon*
Transport: *Nashville*
Dock Landing Ship: *Whidbey Island*
Tank Landing Ships: *Newport, Fairfax County*
Amphibious Ready Group III (with 5th Marine Brigade)

Carrier Group Saratoga
Attack Carrier (CV): *Saratoga*
Aegis Cruiser (CGA): *Philippine Sea* (24+ TH)
Destroyers: *Sampson, Spruance* (TH)
Frigates: *Montgomery, Hart*

Carrier Group Kennedy
Attack Carrier (CV): *John F. Kennedy*
Aegis Cruisers (CGA): *Gates* (24+ TH), *San Jacinto* (100+ TH)
Missile Cruiser (CG): *Mississippi*
Destroyer: *Moosbrugger*
Frigate: *Roberts*
Supply Ships: *Seattle, Sylvania*

Carrier Group Midway
Attack Carrier (CV): *Midway*
Aegis Cruisers (CGA): *Bunker Hill* (24+ TH), *Mobile Bay* (24+ TH)
Destroyers: *Hewitt, Oldendorf*
Frigates: *Curts, Rodney Davis*

Carrier Group Roosevelt
Nuclear Carrier (CVN): *Theodore Roosevelt*
Aegis Cruiser (CGA): *Leyte Gulf* (24+TH)
Missile Cruiser (CG): *Richard K. Turner*
Destroyer: *Caron* (60 TH)
Frigates: *Hawes, Vreeland*
Fleet Oiler: *Platte*
Ammunition Ship: *Nitro*
Supply Ship: *San Diego*

Carrier Group America
Attack Carrier (CV): *America*
Aegis Cruiser (CGA): *Normandy*
Missile Crusier (CG): *Virginia* (8+ TH)
Destroyers: *Preeble, William V. Pratt*
Frigate: *Haklyburton*
Fleet Oiler: *Kalamazoo*
Ammunition Ship: *Santa Barbara*

Carrier Group Ranger
Aircraft Carrier (CV): *Ranger*
Aegis Cruiser (CGA): *Valley Forge, Princeton*
Destroyers: *Will, Foster*
Frigate: *Hammond*
Fleet Oiler: *Kansas City*
Ammunition Ship: *Shasta*

Royal Navy
(United Kingdom)
Destroyers: *York, Gloucester*
Frigates: *Jupiter, Battleaxe*
Minehunters: *Cattisock, Hurworth, Atherstone*
Tanker: *Orangeleaf*
Hospital Ship: *Argus*

Portugal
Supply Ship: *Sao Miguel*, to act as replenishment vessel for British.

Canada
Destroyers: *Athabascan, Terra Nova*
Supply Ship: One

Australia
Destroyer: *Brisbane*
Frigate: *Sydney* (replacing *Adelaide* and *Darwin*)
Supply Ship: *Success*

France
Frigates: *Protet, Commandant Ducuing, Montcalm, Dupleix*
Tanker: *Durance*

Belgium
Frigate: *Wandelaar*
Minesweepers: *Iris, Myosotis*
Support Ship: *Zinnia*

Netherlands
Frigates: *Witte de With, Pieter Florisz*
Support Ship: *Zuiderkruis*

Italy
Frigates: *Orsa, Libeccio, Zeffro*
Corvettes: *Sfinge, Minerva*
Supply Ship: *Stromboli*

Spain
Frigate: *Numancia* (replacing *Santa Maria*)
Corvettes: *Diana, Infanta Cristina* (replacing *Cazadora* and *Descubierta*)

Greece
Frigate: *Elli* (replacing *Limnos*)

US GROUND FORCES

Americans seem to have a national inferiority complex about themselves when it comes to military affairs. Why this is so is a mystery, but it certainly is so. There is a continuous undercurrent of uncertainty and fear about the US military in American thought, as if it is beyond out national ability (or contrary to our national character) to produce an outstanding army. There are the constant nagging doubts that, no matter how much objective evidence is supplied to the contrary, somehow everything will go wrong in battle.

The training will have been unrealistic. The soldiers will be too soft. The weapons won't work; they are either grossly inferior to more modern foreign ones or, if they *are* more modern, then they are "unproven" and will probably be too complex and "high tech" to use. Evidence to the contrary is probably fabricated, and the more overwhelming the evidence, the more obvious the fabrication.

Judgments like these have abounded, and they always will. They are not the product of mean-spirited nay-sayers. (Well, not always, anyway.) Instead, they are the product of our own understandable, *but completely groundless,* sense of national military inferiority.

In fact, Americans have always made outstanding soldiers, to which the historical battle honors of US units give eloquent testimony. The US Army today is probably the best we have ever fielded, and that's saying something. It is the best equipped, best trained, and best led army in our history, and arguably the finest in the world today. It is tough, aggressive, and professional. Perhaps after Operation Desert Storm, its officers and enlisted men and women will receive the honest recognition and credit they are due as outstanding soldiers. Perhaps we will shed a bit of our national inferiority complex. Perhaps.

ARMY ORGANIZATION

US heavy divisions (armored and mechanized) are organized along very similar lines. Each division has 10 maneuver battalions in its line brigades plus one divisional cavalry (mechanized recon) battalion, three artillery battalions, an MLRS battery, one or two helicopter gunship battalions, and a battalion each of engineers and air defense artillery. Armored divisions have six tank battalions and four mechanized battalions, while the proportion is reversed in mechanized divisions. Armored cavalry regiments have

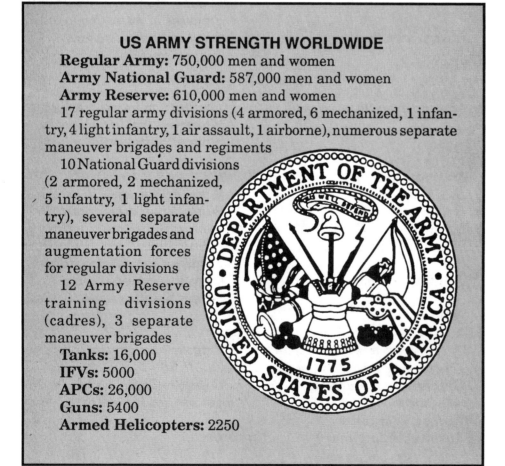

US ARMY STRENGTH WORLDWIDE

Regular Army: 750,000 men and women
Army National Guard: 587,000 men and women
Army Reserve: 610,000 men and women

17 regular army divisions (4 armored, 6 mechanized, 1 infantry, 4 light infantry, 1 air assault, 1 airborne), numerous separate maneuver brigades and regiments

10 National Guard divisions (2 armored, 2 mechanized, 5 infantry, 1 light infantry), several separate maneuver brigades and augmentation forces for regular divisions

12 Army Reserve training divisions (cadres), 3 separate maneuver brigades

Tanks: 16,000
IFVs: 5000
APCs: 26,000
Guns: 5400
Armed Helicopters: 2250

three armored cavalry squadrons (battalions), an air cavalry squadron, and an artillery battalion.

Tank battalions consist of a headquarters company and four tank companies. Each tank company has three platoons of four tanks each, plus two tanks in the headquarters section. The battalion headquarters company has two command tanks, a cavalry platoon with six M3 Bradley cavalry fighting vehicles (CFV, a variant of the M2 IFV), a platoon with six self-propelled heavy mortars, and a variety of support units.

Mechanized battalions are organized along similar lines. The battalion itself consists of a headquarters company, four mechanized infantry companies, and an antiarmor company. The headquarters company is the same as in the tank battalion except that the command section has M2 Bradleys instead of tanks. The infantry companies each have three platoons (three rifle squads, a command group, and four Bradleys each) and a company command group with another Bradley. The antiarmor company has three platoons, each with four M901 Improved TOW vehicles and an M-113 command track, plus a small company headquarters and another M-113.

Helicopter gunship battalions each have a headquarters company and three attack helicopter companies. The headquarters company has supporting units and a few observation and utility helicopters for command and support work. Each attack helicopter company has an attack helicopter platoon of seven gunships (AH-1 Cobras or AH-64 Apaches) and a scout platoon of four observation helicopters (OH-58 Kiowas).

Armored cavalry squadrons have an unusual mixed organization. Each squadron (battalion) has a headquarters troop (two command tanks and supporting units), three cavalry troops, and a tank company, organized just like that of a tank battalion. Each cavalry troop (company) has two scout platoons of six M3 Bradley CFVs each, two tank platoons of four tanks each, a mortar section with two heavy, self-propelled mortars, and a headquarters section with an additional tank. This gives an armored cavalry squadron a total of 43 main battle tanks and 36 CFVs, a very powerful mechanized force.

Artillery battalions consist of three firing batteries, each with two platoons of four guns each, for a total of 24 guns per battalions.

THE MARINES

Unlike the army, the marines still use regiments as tactical units. The marines have brigades, but these are formed for duty separate from a division. A division operates with regiments and complete battalions of supporting arms (tanks, LAVs, etc.) which it allocates to the regiments and battalions as needed.

Instead of corps, the marines use a headquarters called a marine expeditionary force. Originally these were built around division headquarters, but the divisions now are separate entities. (As the 1st and 2nd Divisions and the 1st and 2nd Expeditionary Forces were deployed top the gulf, this caused no end of confusion).

Except for very large operations such as Desert Storm, the expeditionary force normally exercises direct control over marine expeditionary brigades (several rifle battalions plus supporting arms) and marine expeditionary units (a

single marine battalion plus supporting arms). The organization of 2nd Marine Expeditionary Force in Desert Storm is a good example of this.

For very large operations, however, the division headquarters are deployed and directly control their subordinate regiments. The organization of 1st Marine Expeditionary Force is a good example of this.

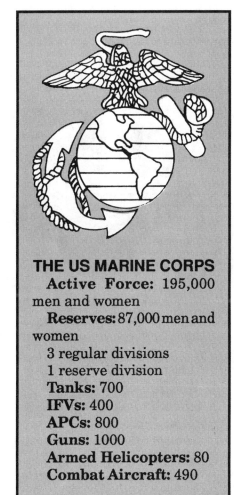

THE US MARINE CORPS
  Active Force: 195,000 men and women
  Reserves: 87,000 men and women
  3 regular divisions
  1 reserve division
  Tanks: 700
  IFVs: 400
  APCs: 800
  Guns: 1000
  Armed Helicopters: 80
  Combat Aircraft: 490

FRENCH & BRITISH GROUND FORCES
NATO ALLIES

FRANCE

The French *Force Action Rapide* (FAR, standing for Rapid Action Force) was formed in 1983 to undertake the same sort of mission as the US Rapid Deployment Force (Central Command). It consists of five divisions of troops: the 9th Marine, 11th Airborne, 27th Alpine, 6th Light Armored, and 4th Airmobile. Its troops are all volunteers (there are legal restrictions on the deployment of French conscripts overseas), and form an elite corps with the French Army.

When the gulf crisis broke out, the French quickly dispatched a small brigade-sized detachment of the 6th Light Armored Division. The rest of the division followed

soon after, but was not considered sufficiently strong to carry out sustained combat against heavy forces. To remedy this, a variety of additional assets were attached to the division from other elements of the FAR, including an airmobile detachment, additional infantry, and more field guns.

The one asset that the FAR has never had, however, is heavy armor. Given the need for a medium tank regiment in the KTO, the French scrambled to re-man the 4th Dragoon Regiment, an AMX-30B2 unit with a European mission, with all-volunteer crews. This was one of the last units of the division to arrive.

The considerably reinforced

group entered action as the Daguet Division.

Daguet Division (French 6th Light Armored Division, Reinforced)

Organic Troops, 6th Light Armored Division

1st Foreign Legion Armored Regiment (35 AMX-10RC)

1st Regiment de Spahis (35 AMX-10RC)

2nd Foreign Legion Infantry Regiment (VAB APCs)

21st Marine Infantry Regiment (VAB APCs)

68th Marine Artillery Regiment (four batteries of towed 155mm howitzers, one battery of Mistral SAM)

6th Foreign Legion Engineer Regiment

From 4th Airmobile Division

5th Combat Helicopter Regiment (10 20mm gunships, 30 AT helicopters with HOT ATGM)

1st Transport Helicopter Regiment

1st Infantry Regiment (airmobile)

From 9th Marine Division

2nd Marine Infantry Regiment (VAB APCs)

Detachment, 3rd Marine Infantry Regiment (269 men)

11th Marine Artillery Regiment (four batteries of towed 155mm howitzers)

From 10th Armored Division

4th Dragoon Regiment (40 AMX-30B2 main battle tanks)

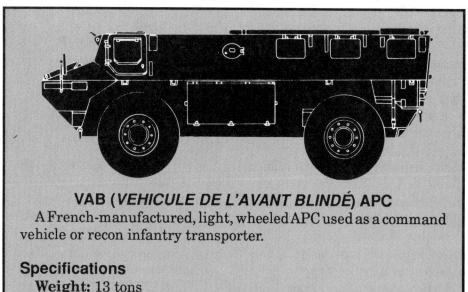

VAB (*VEHICULE DE L'AVANT BLINDÉ*) APC

A French-manufactured, light, wheeled APC used as a command vehicle or recon infantry transporter.

Specifications

Weight: 13 tons
Speed: 92 kph
Gun: 7.62mm
Troops: 10
Armor: 12mm
In Use With: France, Qatar

UNITED KINGDOM

The British contingent to the 3rd Army originally consisted of the 7th Armoured Brigade, although this was later followed by an additional armored brigade, a division headquarters, and several infantry battalions tasked with enemy prisoner of war (EPW) handling.

The British, like the United States, employ an all-volunteer Army with high standards of professionalism and a long tradition of excellence. Although top honors among NATO ground troops are hotly argued, there is no question but that the British should be either at or near the top of the list.

British doctrine differs considerably from US AirLand Battle doctrine, both in detail and in general philosophy. The British have always valued firepower over maneuver, and are trained for a more deliberate style of warfare than the wide, sweeping dash contemplated by 3rd Army. Also, mingling the British with US units to either flank would complicate an already formidable logistical task. To use the British to their best advantage, in a battle suited to their style of combat, they were placed on the inner hinge of VII Corps' swinging arm.

1st Armoured Division
7th Armoured Brigade

Royal Scots Dragoon Guards (57 Challenger MBTs)

Queen's Royal Irish Hussars (57 Challenger MBTs)

1st Staffordshire Infantry (45 Warrior IFVs)

39th Regiment, Royal Engineers

664th Helicopter Squadron (9 Lynx)

10th Air Defense Battery (Javelin)

40th Field Regiment (24 M109 SP howitzers)

4th Armoured Brigade

14/20 King's Hussars (43 Challenger MBTs)

1st Royal Scots Infantry (45 Warrior IFVs)

3rd Royal Fusiliers Infantry (45 Warrior IFVs)

23rd Regiment, Royal Engineers

46th Air Defense Battery (Javelin)

2nd Field Regiment (24 M109 SP howitzers)

Division Troops

16/5 Queen's Royal Lancers Recon Battalion (24 Scorpion, 24 Scimitar, 12 Striker)

4th Army Air Regiment (24 Lynx with TOW, 12 Gazelle)

32nd Heavy Artillery Regiment (16 M109, 12 M110)

29th Heavy Artillery Regiment (12 MLRS)

12th Air Defense Regiment (24 tracked Rapier)

32nd Regiment, Royal Engineers

EPW Handling
Infantry Battalions

1st Coldstream Guards

Royal Highland Fusiliers

King's Own Scottish Borderers

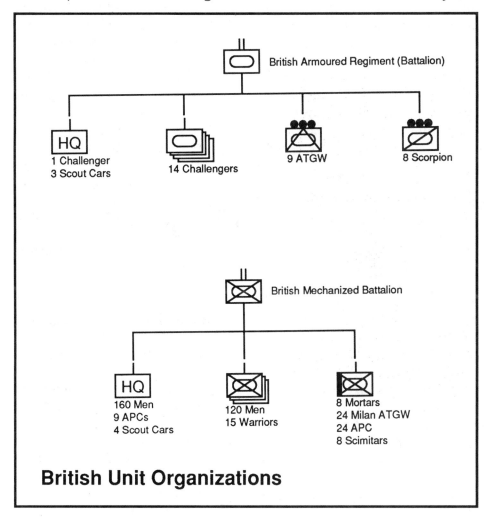

British Armoured Regiment (Battalion)

HQ
1 Challenger
3 Scout Cars

14 Challengers

9 ATGW

8 Scorpion

British Mechanized Battalion

HQ
160 Men
9 APCs
4 Scout Cars

120 Men
15 Warriors

8 Mortars
24 Milan ATGW
24 APC
8 Scimitars

British Unit Organizations

THE JOINT ARAB COMMAND

The Joint Arab Command was built around a solid core of regular units which existed before the ourbreak of hostilities, but it also had a large numbet of odds and ends grafted onto it as the ground war drew nearer. Its organization changed several times, but this section will limit itself to a discussion of the origin of the separate components of the force and its final organization.

THE SAUDI ARMY

The Saudi ground forces are actually two armies in one: the Royal Saudi Land Forces (RSLF) and the Saudi Arabian National Guard (SANG). The second force is not a reserve component, but rather is a tribally recruited paramilitary force, intensely loyal to the king, tasked with border duties and maintenance of the regime. It is well-equipped, but with lighter weapons than the "regulars." It has no tanks of its own, for example, and is mounted in V-150 wheeled APCs instead of tracked APCs or IFVs.

The prewar strength of the RSLF was two armored brigades, four mechanized brigades one infantry brigade, a Royal Guard brigade, two airborne battalions, and five artillery battalions. The SANG had two mechanized brigades.

THE KUWAIT ARMY

Prior to the invasion of Kuwait, the army mustered two armored brigades and a mechanized infantry brigade. These troops were unprepared for hostilities, and resistance from the ground forces was only sporadic. Elements of the 35th Armored Brigade apparently inflicted some losses on the enemy before withdrawing to Saudi Arabia. The 25th and 15th Brigades apparently did not do as well and lost much of their equipment.

In Saudi Arabia, the Kuwaitis accepted delivery on a number of Yugoslavian M-84 tanks ordered before the war and began to rebuild their army. For a country with a population as small as Kuwait's, and much of it under enemy occupation, the number of men placed under arms and committed to the battle was impressive. There has never in history been an army raised in exile containing as high a percentage of the population.

THE PENINSULA SHIELD FORCE

This is a standing military force amounting to a weak division and containing contingents from all of the Gulf Coopertive Council states. In peacetime it consists of a Saudi brigade and a composite brigade made up of troops from Bahrain, Oman, Qatar, and the United Arab Emirates. Upon the outbreak of war all of the contingents were reinforced and formed into task forces with Saudi, Kuwaiti, and other African and Asian contingents.

SYRIA

Syria sent the 9th Armored Division, equipped with T-62 tanks and BMP IFVs, to serve with the Joint Arab Force. As with the other Arab forces, political considerations limited the employmnt of the force to Kuwait proper. For a time it was attached to the Egyptian II Corps, but later served directly under the Joint Forces Command–North.

EGYPT

Egypt provided more ground troops than any other Coalition member expect for the United States and Saudi Arabia. Two strong divisions were sent along with a highly trained Ranger regiment (brigade-strength). In terms of experience and training, the Egyptians were probably the best of the Arab forces. The Egyptians fought as a unified corps, but under the command of the Joint Forces Command–North.

THE JOINT ARAB FORCE AT WAR

By the start of the offensive, the Joint Forces Command was divided into two corps-size elements and a Forward Forces Command, which served as a covering force for the buildup and assembly of troops before the attack. The following is a detailed order of battle of the Joint Forces Command during the ground campaign.

FORWARD FORCES COMMAND

RSLF 5th Airborne Battalion
SANG King Faisal Brigade (41st

& 42nd Battalions)
Pakistani 7th Armored Brigade

JOINT FORCES COMMAND–EAST
Direct Control
RSLF 10th Mechanized Brigade (with M-60 tanks) (–1 mechanized battalion)
UAE Mechanized Battalion (with AMX-30 tanks)
Northern Omani Brigade (reinforced)

Task Force Othman
RSLF 8th Mechanized Brigade (with M60 tanks)
Bahraini Motorized Infantry Company
Kuwaiti "Al Fatah" Brigade
Kuwaiti 2/15 Mech Battalion

Task Force Bakar
SANG 2nd Mechanized Brigade

Task Force Tariq
Royal Saudi Marine Battalion
Moroccan 6th Mechanized Battalion
Senegalese 1st Infantry Battalion

Reserve and Support
RSLF 14th Field Artillery Battalion
RSLF 18th Missile Battalion
RSLF 2nd Antitank Company
RSLF 6th Target Acquisition Battery
Qatari Mechanized Battalion TF (with AMX-30 tanks)
1st East Bengal Infantry Battalion

JOINT FORCES COMMAND–NORTH
Syrian
45th Commando Brigade
122nd, 183rd, 824th SF Battalions
One artillery battalion

One antitank battalion

Syrian 9th Armored Division
33rd, 43rd Armored Brigades (T-62)
52nd Mechanized Brigade (T-62/BMP)
89th Artillery Regiment
79th Antiaircraft Brigade

Task Force Muthana
RSLF 20th Mechanized Brigade (with M60 tanks)
Kuwaiti 35th Mechanized Brigade (with M84 tanks)

Task Force Sa'ad
RSLF 4th Armored Brigade (AMX-30)
Kuwaiti 15th Infantry Brigade

Egyptian II Corps
3rd Mechanized Division
10th, 114th Mechanized Brigades (M113/M60)
23rd Armored Brigade (M60/M113)
39th Artillery Brigade (M109)
126th Antiaircraft Artillery Brigade
4th Armored Division
2nd, 3rd Armored Brigades (M60/M113)
6th Mechanized Brigade (M113/M60)
4th Artillery Brigade (M109)
1st Ranger Regiment (three battalions and support troops)

Command Support and Reserve
Saudi Attack Aviation Battalion
RSLF 15th MLRS Battalion
RSLF 7th Target Acquisition Company
RSLF Antitank Company
RSLF 4th Airborne Battalion
Czech NBC Defense Company
Kuwaiti "Haq" Brigade
Kuwaiti "Khulud" Brigade

THE OTHER ALLIES
Bangladesh Brigade (6000 Men): Garrison in Mecca
Bangladesh 1st East Bengal Infantry Battalion: With Joint Forces Command–East
Moroccan 6th Mechanized Battalion (1200 Men with M113 APCs): With TF Tariq, Joint Forces Command–East
Senegalese Infantry Battalion (481 Men Commanded by Col. Senyi): With TF Tariq, Joint Forces Command–East
Niger Infantry Battalion (500 Men): With Joint Forces Command–North
Pakistani 7th Armored Brigade: With Forward Forces Command
Pakistani Infantry Battalion: Garrison in UAE
Czech Chem Defense Company: With Joint Forces Command–North
South Korea Medical Unit: With Joint Forces Command–East
Czech Field Hospital
New Zealand Field Hospital
Dutch Field Hospital
Polish Field Hospital

STRUCTURE OF THE ARMY
IRAQI GROUND FORCES

Iraqi corps function as the largest permanent field headquarters in the army. Prior to the invasion of Kuwait, there were seven permanent army corps (numbered I through VII) and the Republican Guard Forces Command, which was about corps strength. Each corps had one armored or mechanized division and five infantry divisions, on the average. This could vary considerably, however.

Following the invasion of Kuwait, a large number of additional divisions were mobilized (many of them at very reduced strength) and several new corps headquarters were established to control them. The Republican Guard was expanded and divided into two corps (I Guards and II Guards) while three more corps were added to the regular army (VIII Tank, IX Reserve, and X Reserve). The first of these controlled five tank and mechanized divisions stripped from other corps, while the last two controlled groups of newly formed reserve divisions.

The largest unit in the Iraqi army with a fixed organization is the division. A division consists of three maneuver brigades (infantry, armor, or mechanized), an artillery brigade, and a variety of supporting battalions and companies.

The three principal types of divisions in the Iraqi Army are infantry, mechanized, and armor. The infantry and mechanized organizations are shown in the two accompanying diagrams. Armored divisions use the same organization as mechanized divisions with two exceptions: The armored division has two armored and one mechanized brigade (instead of the opposite in a mechanized division), and the armored division had no antitank battalion.

COMBAT UNITS

Each battalion in the division consists of three companies, each of which is in turn made up of three platoons. Tank platoons have four tanks (14 in the company, 44 in the battalion). Artillery platoons have two guns, howitzers, or multiple rocket launchers (six in the battery, as artillery companies are called, 18 in the battalion). Infantry platoons have three 10-man rifle squads and a small weapons squad with a light machinegun and an RPG-7 rocket launcher.

In some mechanized units, the company has a 60mm mortar platoon (two mortars) in addition to its three rifle platoons. Otherwise, there are no mortars or heavy weapons in a battalion other than those of the weapons squads in each platoon.

Republican Guard units are stronger than this. Each tank battalion has four companies instead of three (60 tanks instead of 44), each company has a platoon of 82mm mortars, and each rifle squad has its own light machinegun and RPG-7. Many special forces units may be organized and equipped similarly.

SUPPORT UNITS

In addition to the combat units shown on the chart, brigades and divisions have a number of non-combat support units. Each brigade has a supply company and a chemical decontamination platoon. Each division has a supply-and-transport battalion, a medical battalion, a communication battalion, military police company, and chemical decontamination company. All armored and mechanized divisions

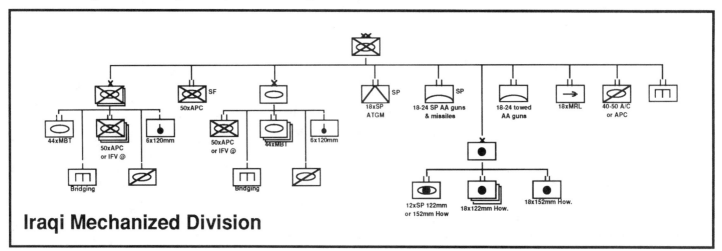

Iraqi Mechanized Division

also have a technical engineering battalion in addition to their combat engineer battalion. This unit contains heavy bridging and road construction equipment needed to sustain mobility in difficult terrain.

IRAQI SPECIAL FORCES

In the United States Army, and in most armies for that matter, the term *special forces* implies an irregular of commando-type mission. US special forces, for example, specialize in training indigenous troops in light infantry and guerrilla-type warfare, and excel at those sorts of missions themselves.

Iraqi special forces are completely different. The bulk of Iraq's army is infantry, but the concentration of the best troops in armored, mechanized, and Republican Guard formations left the infantry divisions incapable of mounting much of an offensive. To maximize the effectiveness of what quality troops were left to the infantry, divisions began forming special forces companies during the war with Iran. The closest historical parallel to these companies would be the German *Stosstruppen* of late World War I.

In that conflict, Germany also faced the problem of coaxing offensive operations out of depleted and battle-weary infantry formations, and did so by concentrating the very best troops of a division in its *Stosskompanie*. Each of these companies received additional training and was given extra weapons to carry out its mission, which was to spearhead the division's attack.

The Iraqi special forces companies are nearly identical in concept. They are the best troops in the division and receive the best weapons. If the division has any APCs, they are usually given to the special forces detachment. By the end of the war with Iran most divisions had a full special forces battalion and a few divisions had two or three grouped into a brigade. Each corps also has one or two special forces brigades.

In defense, the division's special forces battalion is usually grouped with its tank battalion as a mobile and hard-hitting reserve force. In the attack most of the tanks support the main infantry attack, but a company or more would be held back along with the special forces battalion as an exploitation force. The Iraqi Army is not proficient at battlefield reconnaissance, and so the actual infantry attack is used to find weak spots. Once the broad front attack identifies a weak spot, the heavily armed special forces battalion, reinforced with tanks, is committed to beak through and exploit.

An additional function of special forces detachments is to ensure the loyalty of regular troops and to keep them in the line when times get tough. This may be the origin of the reports of so-called "execution battalions."

INFANTRY PLATOON FIREPOWER

The following chart compares the manpower and weapons of a US mechanized infantry platoon equipped with Bradley IFVs to an Iraqi mechanized platoon equipped with BMP IFVs. Virtually all US infantry is mechanized and mounted in Bradleys. Most Iraqi infantry is leg-mobile, and only about 15% of the mechanized battalions have BMPs; the rest use APCs armed only with machineguns.

Category	US	Iraq
Troops	33	36
IFVs	4	4
AR	24	32
GL	7	0
SAW	6	1
GPMG	3	0
ATRL	15	1
ATGM	3	0

Notes: *IFV:* Infantry fighting vehicle (US Bradley with 25mm chaingun and TOW-II launcher, Iraqi BMP-1 with 73mm low-velocity gun and AT-3 Sagger launcher) *AR:* Assault rifle (US M16, Iraqi AKM) *GL:* Grenade launcher (US M203) *SAW:* Squad Automatic Weapon (US M249 SAW, Iraqi RPK) *GPMG:* General-purpose machinegun (US M60) *ATRL:* Antitank rocket launcher (US AT-4, Iraqi RPG-7) *ATGM:* Antitank guided missile (US Dragon).

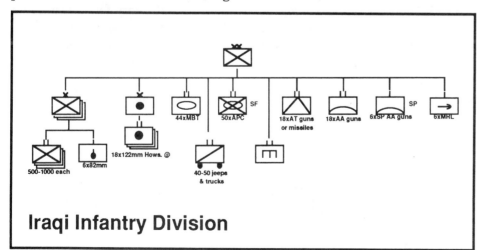

Iraqi Infantry Division

THE IRAQI AIR FORCE

Iraq did possess the sixth largest air force in the world. Their newest Soviet combat aircraft were believed to be among the best in the world. Yet not a single Coalition aircraft was shot down by an Iraqi fighter, not a single Coalition soldier was killed by air attack. Was the Iraqi Air Force overrated?

FORGED IN FIRE

Despite a lot of reasonably good equipment, the Iraqi Air Force impressed few observers before and during the first years of the Iraq-Iran War, but like the Iraqi Army it was tempered by that long war.

1980: The Iraqi Air Force opened Iraq's war with Iran with an overambitious attack on 10 Iranian Air Force bases. They apparently overestimated the amount of damage each of their aircraft could inflict and did not realize how difficult aircraft parked in revetments were to destroy. The Iranian Air Force then launched attacks on Iraqi air bases. The Iraqis learned the hard way what easy targets their unrevetted aircraft were. After losing much of their force, they withdrew their surviving aircraft to bases near Jordan. During the early months of the war, when the Iraqi Army's chances for success were the greatest, the Iraqi Air Force had lost control of the air over the battlefield and over much of Iraq.

1982: Modern combat jets consume spare parts like the family car consumes gas. Iran was not as successful as Iraq at getting around the international arms embargo that had been imposed on both nations, so gradually fewer and fewer Iranian aircraft could fly and the Iraqi Air Force eventually returned to the fray.

1983: The effectiveness of the Iraqi Air Force received a big boost when Iraq gave the Soviets information on the US improved HAWK antiaircraft missile, or possibly a captured battery, and the Soviets gave them in return 100 jamming pods.

1984: The Iraqi Air Force was also getting help from France. Impressed by the Argentine success against the British during the Falklands/Malvinas War, it started attacking Iranian tankers with excellent antiship missiles. If Iraq could cut off Iran's oil income, it could prevent Iran from buying additional weapons. Iraq achieved partial success. Also in 1984, the Iraqi Air Force received 5000 sophisticated combined effects cluster bombs (containing many antipersonnel, antiarmor, and incendiary bomblets in each bomb) from Chile.

1985: The Iraqi Air Force continued its offensive against Iran's oil income as the Iraqi Army continued to stay on the defensive and attempted to recover from heavy casualties.

1986: The Iraqi Army was almost defeated in several battles, but the Iraqi Air Force was used as a kind of a final reserve, being thrown into the battle when Iraqi lines were shattered. This bought time for the Iraqi Army to reform. Attacks on Iran oil exports became more effective, so Iran began exporting oil from Larak in the south of the gulf. Iraqi Air Force F-1s attacked Larak, apparently after in-air refueling. (*Note:* Larak is 150 nautical miles further from Iraq the Saudi capital of Riyadh.) About this time, the Iraqi Air Force received a computerized wargame from a US company that allowed them to assess the probable losses and effects from attacks on various Iranian targets. More types of targets began to be hit; the pattern seemed to be intended to shake the confidence of the Iranian people in their government.

1987: Iraqi Air Force kept up the pressure on Iran while the Iraqi Army remained mostly on the defensive.

1988: The Iraqi Air Force displayed increasing skill and versatility in its strategic attacks on Iranian targets. It began using laser-seeking smart missiles. The Iraqi Air Force did not play an impressive role in the successful offensives by the Iraqi Army that year. While the Iraqi Air Force had some good attack aircraft, very few coordinated AirLand attacks were made. Possible explanations include:

- The Soviet wargame the Iraqi Army used to plan its ground offensives does not easily depict air support.
- Iraqi pilots considered Iraqi antiaircraft gunners too trigger happy.
- Soviet attack helicopters seemed to be taking over the role of joint attack on surface forces.

BETWEEN THE WARS

The Iraqi Air Force continued to increase in sophistication and capabilities between the end of the war with Iran and the invasion of Kuwait. The Iraqis obtained an airborne surveillance and control capability by mounting state-of-the-art French radar in a Soviet transport. Iraq began receiving the MiG-29 Fulcrum before the war with Iran ended and those deliveries continued. The Fulcrum is believed by many to be potentially among the most effective air to air fighters in the world. (It is also believed, however, that Iraq received an "export version" with a less-capable radar.)

BASING STRUCTURE

(See the map on page 100.) The ability of the Iraqi Air Force to learn never was more clear than in how its basing evolved during the Iran-Iraq War. During the early fight for control of the air, the Iraqis had seen how much more vulnerable unrevetted aircraft were. They quickly began building revetments. The Iraqis also obtained satellite reconnaissance of Iranian airfields and learned how useful it was to know where your adversary's aircraft are. First, they put simple roofs on their revetments, then they began building very hard aircraft shelters (they were then impregnable with nonnuclear weapons). They also hardened the command and control structure needed to control this force.

At each base there were more covered revetments or shelters than their normal complement of aircraft. This allowed the Iraqis to shift their air effort to different parts of the country without this being discovered by reconnaissance satellites.

ASSESSMENT

Based upon past performance and on-hand equipment, an assessment of the Iraqi Air Force made at the time of the invasion of Kuwait would have probably made these points:

While the Iraqis have the equipment necessary to do a credible job defending their airspace they have had this equipment for a relatively short period of time and most pilots are probably not proficient yet. Besides, the Soviets are training them to fly the MiG-29 and Soviet training makes pilots dependent on instructions from a controller. The US Air Force should see to it that all controllers rapidly go off the air.

While they have a fair amount of aircraft capable of ground attack, this is not a significant threat in that they lack the procedures to plan joint air/ground attacks and have little experience in carrying out such attacks.

However, Iraq possesses a cadre of battle-tested pilots and equipment that has demonstrated an ability to attack strategic targets with skill and resourcefulness.

So out of Iraq's 700 aircraft air force the only significant threat comes from 75 Mirage F-1 and 70 MiG-27 Floggers. Both aircraft can be refueled in the air from Iraqi-modified AN-12 transports. Both have demonstrated the ability to use sophisticated laser designation systems and laser-seeking, air-to-surface smart missiles.

Little wonder the first forces the US sent to the gulf were two squadrons of F-15 Eagle fighters and five E-3 Sentry AWACS.

IRAQI AIR ORDER OF BATTLE

It is unclear whether a precise order of battle of the Iraqi Air Force as of August 1, 1990 exists outside of Iraq. Not all sales to Baghdad were made public and not all losses in the Iran-Iraq War were acknowledged. The following are best guesses. Aircraft are listed by how crews train. The MiG-25 is counted twice.

GULF WAR
F A C T   B O O K
The Forces

Fighters
  MiG-29s: 40-80
  MiG-25s: 18 (most may be used for reconnaissance)
  MiG-23s: 20
  MiG-21s: 105
  F-7s: 20

Fighter/Attack
  MiG-17s: 30

Attack
  Su-25s: 20
  Su-20s: 30
  Su-7s: 50
  F-6s: 20
  Hunters: 30

Bombers
  Su-24s: 10
  Mirage F1s: 100 (perhaps one-quarter train as fighters)
  MiG-23/27s: 70
  Il-28s: 10
  Tu-22s: 7
  Tu-16s: 12

Reconnaissance
  MiG-25s: 18 (some may be used as fighters)

Surveillance and Control
  Il-75s: 2?

Tankers
  An-2s: 4

Transports
  About 80 consisting of a wide variety of types.

THE IRAQI ARMY
ORDER OF BATTLE

The Iraqi Army ended the Iran-Iraq War with a strength approaching one million men, and Saddam continued the military buildup after the war. In August, the army was organized in seven corps and a Republican Guard. A corps typically had one armored or mechanized division, five or six infantry divisions, and several separate brigades of combat and support troops. (See map on page 97.) The Republican Guard was considerably stronger than that.

The intial invasion of Kuwait was conducted by the Republican Guard, but that force was soon withdrawn and replaced with infantry divisions drawn from the southern corps. As hostilities apporached, two corps headquarters (III and IV) were moved into Kuwait to control the infantry there, and the other corps on the Iranian frontier sidestepped south to cover the gap. VII Corps was apparently stripped of the majority of its troops, but probably became active controlling the defenses in southern Iraq.

Most of the heavy divisions (armored and mechanized) were stripped from the other corps and concentrated in central Kuwait under a new corps headquarters, VIII Tank. At the same time a large number of new divisions were formed from mobilized reservists and young volunteers, and these were grouped temporarily under the IX and X Reserve Corps. The IX Corps moved south with a gaggle of hastily raised reserve divisions while X Corps remained in the north to supervise additional training. IX Reserve Corps contributed at least four reserve divisions to the improvised southwestern defenses (45th, 47th, 48th, and 49th) and may have remained active to supervise the western end of the line. (See map on page 98.)

On the eve of the Allied offensive, the Iraqi Army commanded impressive numbers of troops.

Total Strength
1,200,000 men

Equipment
5500 main battle tanks
1000 IFVs
1000 armored recon vehicle
7000 APCs
3000 towed guns
500 SP guns
200 multiple-rocket launchers
4000 air defense guns
350 long-range SAMs
100 surface-to-surface missiles
160 armed attack helicopters

Deployment
(See map on page 99.) Formations deployed in the Kuwaiti Theater of Operations are listed in bold, and have more detailed information provided.

I Corps (northern Kurdistan)
  6 regular infantry divisions
  8 reserve infantry divisions
II Corps (southern Iranian border)
  5 regular infantry divisions
III Corps (Kuwaiti-Saudi border)
  10 regular infantry divisions (7, 8, 14, 16, 18, 21, 26, 29, 30, 36)
IV Corps (Kuwaiti Coastal Defense)
  5 regular infantry divisions (2, 11, 19, unknown, unknown)
  2 reserve infantry divisions (42, unknown)
V Corps (northern Iranian border)
  5 regular infantry divisions
VI Corps (Syrian border)
  6 regular infantry divisions
VII Corps (southern Iraq)
  3 regular infantry divisions (25, 27, 31)
  2 reserve infantry divisions (47, 48)
  1 armored division (12)
VIII Tank Corps (central Kuwait)
  3 armored divisions (3, 6, 10)
  2 mechanized divisions (5, 51)
IX Reserve Corps (southwestern Iraq)
  1 regular infantry division (26)
  2 reserve infantry divisions (45, 49)
X Reserve Corps (central Iraq)
  8 reserve infantry divisions
Republican Guard Forces

THE IRAQI NAVY
5 frigates
32 patrol boats
6 amphibious ships

Iraq also had a fleet of 13 modern ships on order from Italy, but these were never delivered. The entire Iraqi fleet was sunk or rendered combat-ineffective by air power during the course of the war.

Command

  2 Republican Guard armored divisions (1 Gd, 2 Gd)

  1 reserve armored division (unknown)

  1 Republican Guard mechanized division (3 Gd)

  3 Republican Guard motorized infantry divisions (4 Gd, 6 Gd, 7 Gd)

  1 Republican Guard special forces division (8 Gd)

  Central Reserve

    2 regular infantry divisions

    1 RG motorized division

    1 mechanized division

IRAQ'S REPUBLICAN GUARD

The Republican Guard was originally intended to provide President Saddam Hussein with a body of troops with unquestioning loyalty. As the principal means of presidential succession in Iraq had become coup and murder, these troops were more political than military. They originally consisted of three brigades recruited from Tikrit, Hussein's home town in northern Iraq.

Although the comparisons between Hitler and Hussein can be pushed too far, the original purpose of the Republican Guard was very similar to the SS: a small, politically reliable paramilitary force

IRAQI PREWAR TANK STRENGTHS (ESTIMATED)	
Tank	*Quantity*
T-54/55	1400
Type 59	500
Type 69	1000
T-62	1600
T-72	1000
Total	5500

inteded to serve as the ruler's personal armed bodyguard. Its subsequent growth has been similar as well. Just as the SS later became a significant part of the German armed forces, absorbed a majority of its best equipment, and formed a heavily mechanized *corps d'elite*, so also did the Republican Guard.

In 1986, the Guard began expanding into a major combat force by means of transfers of selected veteran cadres from the regulars and the addition of thousands of politically sympathetic young volunteers, many of them students. By the end of Iraq's war with Iran, the Guard had expanded to a total of 25 maneuver brigades, its current strength.

Guards units were lavishly equipped by Iraqi standards. Each brigade was self-contained and included a full artillery battalion (18 155mm howitzers) in addition to its brigade mortar battery. Infantry squads had the normal 10 men, but each squad had its own light machinegun and RPG-7 rocket launcher (as opposed to one of each per platoon in regular army units). Tank battalions had four companies instead of three (total of 60 tanks instead of 44). Most of the T-72s, T-62s, and BMPs were assigned to Guard units, and the motorized divisions had a number of APCs and extra tanks.

Iraqi Guards divisions had the standard three-brigade organization except for the 5th "Baghdad" Division. This division, the permanent garrison of the capital, had four brigades and was sometimes divided into two mini-divisions of two brigades each. This was the only division of the Republican Guard which was not committed to the Kuwaiti Theater of Operations.

GULF WAR FACT BOOK
The Forces

IRAQI SUPPLIERS OF LIGHT AFVS
Recon Vehicles
Brazil: EE-3 *Jararaca*, EE-9 Cascavel
France: ERC-90, AML-60, AML-90
Hungary: FUG-70
USSR: BRDM-2
Armored Personnel Carriers
Brazil: EE-11 *Urutu*
China: Type 63
Czechoslovakia: OT-62, OT-63, BVP-1
Egypt: *Walid*
France: Panhard M-3
USSR: BTR-40, BTR-50, BTR-60, BMP-1

The distinctive insignia of the Iraqi Republican Guard is a red triangle worn as a shoulder patch.

Republican Guard Order of Battle

  1st Armored Division "Hammurabi"

  2nd Armored Division "Medina"

  3rd Mechanized Division "Tawakalna"

  4th Motorized Division "Al Faw"

  5th Motorized Division "Baghdad"

  6th Motorized Division "Nebuchadnezzar"

  7th Motorized Division "Adnan"

  8th Special Forces Division

COALITION ORDER OF BATTLE

US 3RD ARMY

2nd Marine Expeditionary Force (Afloat)
4th Marine Expeditionary Brigade
5th Marine Expeditionary Brigade
13th Marine Expeditionary Unit

Forward Forces Command
Saudi King Faisal Brigade (National Guard)
Pakistani 7th Armored Brigade

Joint Forces Command East
Saudi 10th Mechanized Brigade
UAE Mechanized Battalion
North Oman Brigade
Task Force Othman
   Saudi 8th Mechanized, Kuwaiti "Fatah" Brigades

Task Force Abu Bakar (Saudi 2nd National Guard Brigade)
Task Force Tariq
   Saudi Marine, Moroccan 6th Mechanized, and Senegal Battalions
   Reserves:
   Qatari Mechanized Battalion, 1st East Bengal Infantry Battalion

1st Marine Expeditionary Force
1st Marine Division
   1st, 3rd, 4th, and 7th Marine Regiments
   11th Marine (Artillery) Regiment
2nd Marine Division
   6th and 8th Marine Regiments
   10th Marine (Artillery) Regiment
   1st "Tiger" Brigade, 2nd Armored Division

Joint Forces Command North
Syrian 4th Commando Brigade
Syrian 9th Armored Division
    33rd and 43rd Armored, 52nd Mechanized Brigades
Task Force Muthana
    Saudi 20th Mechanized, Kuwaiti 35th Mechanized Brigades
Task Force Sa'ad
    Saudi 4th Armored, Kuwaiti 15th Infantry Brigades
Reserves:
Kuwaiti "Haq" and "Khulud" Brigades

Egyptian II Corps
Egyptian 3rd Mechanized Division
    23rd Armored, 10th and 114th Mechanized Brigades
Egyptian 4th Armored Division
    2nd and 3rd Armored, 6th Mechanized Brigades
Egyptian 1st Ranger Regiment

US VII Corps
1st Cavalry Division (Armored)
    1st and 2nd Brigades
1st Infantry Division (Mechanized)
    1st and 2nd Brigades
    3rd Brigade, 2nd Armored Division (attached)
1st British Armoured Division
    4th, 7th Armoured Brigades

3rd Armored Division
    1st, 2nd, 3rd Brigades
1st Armored Division
    1st, 2nd, 3rd Brigades
2nd Armored Cavalry Regiment
42nd, 72nd 142nd, 210th Field Artillery Brigades
7th Engineer Brigade
11th Aviation Brigade
14th Military Police Brigade

US XVIII Corps
24th Infantry Division (Mechanized)
    1st, 2nd Brigades
    197th Infantry Brigade (Mechanized) (attached)
101st Air Assault Division
    327th, 502nd, 187th Air Assault Regiments
82nd Airborne Division
    325th, 504th, 505th Parachute Regiments
French 6th Light Armored Division
3rd Armored Cavalry Regiment
18th Airborne, 75th, 196th, 212th and 214th Field Artillery Brigades
20th Engineer Brigades
12th and 18th Aviation Brigades
16th, 89th, and 800th MP Brigades

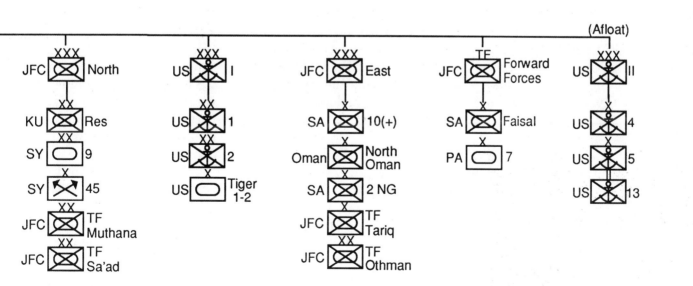

GETTING THERE
STRATEGIC MOBILITY

When President Bush ordered US forces into the gulf a decade of preparations stood behind that decision. Starting shortly after the 1979 Soviet invasion of Afghanistan, the Rapid Deployment Joint Task Force, and later its successor, the United States Central Command (usually called CENTCOM), began planning and wargaming moves into the region. The speed of that move during Desert Shield was a product of those preparations.

Strategic mobility means more than being able to get to a crisis area; forces must be able to unload and fight for as long as necessary. The US military talks about a strategic mobility triad of airlift, sealift, and prepositioning. A more comprehensive description might be a triad of pairs: infrastructure—ports and bases; lift—air and sea; and prepositioning—land-based and sea-based.

INFRASTRUCTURE

Ports: CENTCOM quickly saw there was not enough airport and seaport capacity in the region to rapidly unload arriving transports and freighters.

Bases: CENTCOM also saw there were too few airfields to operate most of the US combat aircraft it was planning to use.

CENTCOM pursued similar strategies to reduce both infrastructure problems. It worked to secure foreign aid so some area governments could build facilities that would also be useful for US forces, if needed. The wealthiest governments in the area were encouraged to overbuild facilities. (Saudi Arabia built five air bases, each almost large enough to accommodate the entire Saudi Air Force.) During Desert Shield there were some bottlenecks and some overcrowded flightlines, but problems were much smaller then they would have been in 1980.

LIFT

Airlift: The Military Airlift Command (MAC) did not possess enough airlift to meet the US's global or even CENTCOM's needs. Several initiatives during the years of the "Reagan buildup" added to Air Force

lift capabilities. The Air Force also gained access to additional capacity through an old program, the Civil Reserve Air Fleet (CRAF). Under this program, the Air Force can borrow civilian airliners and flight crews. While available aircraft could easily carry all the troops needed, there were relatively few commercial airliners equipped to carry cargo. This began to change with the rise of the overnight delivery industry. The Air Force also paid to modify airliners so they could quickly switch to carrying cargo.

Sealift: The Military Sealift Command (MSC) did not come close to possessing enough sealift to meet overall US or CENTCOM needs. In the past this was not a serious problem, as the Navy would call on the US merchant fleet through the Sealift Readiness Program. However, the US merchant fleet was shrinking. The ships that remained tended to be large container ships requiring specialized cargo handling equipment that was usually not available in CENTCOM's area. The US Navy acquired some fast cargo vessels that could unload at austere ports and worked to reduce the time needed to bring old cargo ships out of mothballs.

On 1 October 1986 the US Transportation Command (TRANSCOM) was established to ensure all US lift assets worked together effectively. By all reports they worked.

PREPOSITIONING

Land Based: CENTCOM could not know exactly where in the

THE NAVY AND STRATEGIC MOBILITY

The US Navy is intrinsically strategically mobile over the world's oceans and totally immobile inland. While the speed of the buildup by the US Army and US Air Force was constrained by strategic mobility factors, the Naval buildup was constrained principally by the speed of its ships. However, the shallow, restricted waters of the gulf hindered carrier operations while keeping carriers in more open waters forced aircraft to operate at extreme range.

STRATEGIC MOBILITY OPTIONS

Airlift
- Most expensive option
- Very fast
- Very flexible
- Limited cargo capacity
- Mostly airfield dependent
- CRAF aircraft and KC-10 need specialized unloading equipment

Sealift
- Least expensive option
- Slow to very slow
- Some flexibility
- Huge cargo capacity (The average ship carries the equivalent of 240 C-5 loads.)
- Mostly seaport dependent
- Most civilian ships need specialized offloading equipment

Land-Based Prepositioning
- Expensive
- Requires permission of host government
- Requires marry-up with troops
- Lacks flexibility
- Reduces lift requirements
- Vulnerable to enemy attack

Sea-Based Prepositioning
- Second most expensive
- Requires marry-up with troops
- Some flexibility
- Partially seaport dependent
- Reduces lift requirements
- After unloading, ships can be used for sealift
- Vulnerable to weather and enemy attack; can be sunk

region it would fight. Also, for political reasons several local governments did not give CENTCOM permission to preposition.

Sea Based: As a partial solution, CENTCOM originated the concept of prepositioning on ships. At the beginning of the crisis these ships could proceed to a port close to where they were needed.

When using this method, most prepositioned stocks would be at the wrong locations, but it was far faster to shuttle supplies to the correct base then to bring supplies all the way from the states.

THE AIRLIFTERS
C-141B Starlifter

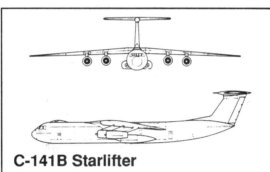

C-141B Starlifter

Crew: 5

Average Speed: 415 knots

Average Range: 3500 miles (unrefueled)

Payload: 13 pallets, 89,000 lbs max (now restricted to 75,000) or a variety of vehicles, or 200 troops, or 153 paratroopers, or 103 litter patients with attendants

Runway Min.: 6000 ft. (average crew)

Inventory: 266

Since 1965 the Starlifter has been the workhorse of military airlift. Two-hundred-and-eighty-five were built. In the early 1980s the fleet was modified to carry three additional pallets and an in air refueling system added.

C-5A/B Galaxy

Crew: 5

Average Speed: 430 knots

Average Range: 3500 miles (unrefueled)

Payload: 75 troops or 36 pallets, 291,000 lbs max or a variety of vehicles or 1 M1 tank or 270 additional troops

Runway Min.: 6000 ft. (average crew)

Inventory: C-5As 89/C-5Bs 50

Operational since 1970, the C-5A has carried cargos no other aircraft could handle. The utility of the C-5A's ability to refuel in the air was aptly demonstrated by the airlift to Israel during the 1973 Arab-Israeli War. The usefulness of this capability of the C-4A contributed to the decision to modify the C-141As so they could be air refueled also. In large part due to the strategic mobility shortfall, 50 more modern C-5B were added to the fleet in the late 1980s.

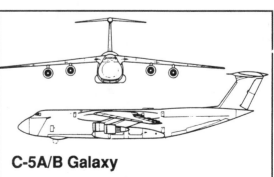

C-5A/B Galaxy

C-130 Hercules (a.k.a. Herky Bird)

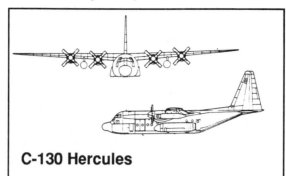

C-130 Hercules

Crew: 5
Average Speed: 270 knots
Average Range: 2500 miles
Payload: 5 pallets, 50,000 lbs max or 92 troops or 64 paratroopers or 74 litter patients
Runway Min.: 3000 ft. (average crew)
Inventory: 492

Officially a "tactical" transport, the Herk's versatility has made it a legend in its own time. Still in production almost 40 years after it first flew, the C-130 may well be the most widely used aircraft in history. It is easier to count the air forces that do *not* fly the Hercules. During Desert Storm the C-130 first moved CENT-COM's prepositioned equipment from where it was to where it was really needed and then hauled cargo from Europe and the Far East.

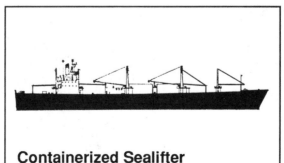

Containerized Sealifter

KC-10A Extender

Crew: 4
Average Speed: 465 knots
Average Range: 4370 miles
Payload: 27 pallets, 170,000 lbs max and 75 passengers
Runway Min.: 7000 ft. (average crew)
Inventory: 59

Based on the commercial DC-10, this "off the shell" aircraft entered service in 1981. The pri-

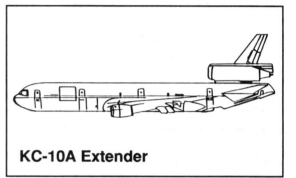

KC-10A Extender

mary mission of the Extender is to enhance strategic mobility of military aircraft. It does this by combining the roles of transport and aerial tanker. A fighter unit's maintenance personnel can deploy aboard a KC-10 while the unit's aircraft fly in the same formation and refuel in flight from the KC-10.

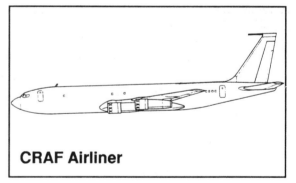

CRAF Airliner

CRAF Airliners

While there is a host of

different aircraft in the CRAF, some generalizations are valid. They are not air refuelable. They require very long runways. Relatively few can haul cargo, and because of their low-wing, high-cargo door design, these need specialized material handling equipment only found at major airports.

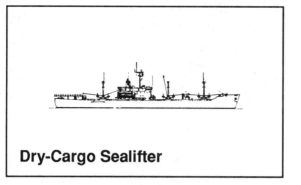

Dry-Cargo Sealifter

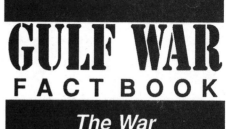
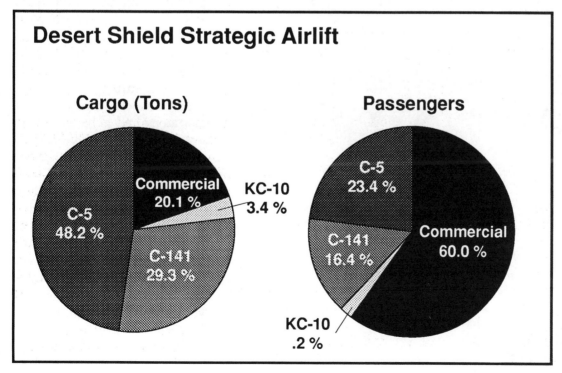

Roll-On/Roll-Off

THE SEALIFTERS
Containerized

The efficiency of this type of ship has resulted in it being by far the most common cargo vessel today. Unfortunately, many ports the military may need to deploy do not have the special equipment needed to unload such ships. Even where such equipment exists it could be disabled by enemy action.

Dry-Cargo

When most people think of a freighter this is the type of ship they think of. While it requires a port to unload, small ports with the most common unloading equipment will do. While the numbers of this type of ship are declining in commercial service, it makes up the bulk of the US's mothballed fleet.

Roll-On/Roll-Off (Ro-Ro)

This type of ship allows vehicles to simply drive on and drive off. It is very popular with military planners, because it can be easily loaded and unloaded from almost any dock without specialized and

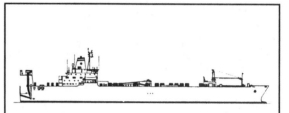

Lighter-Aboard-Ship

vulnerable equipment. Unfortunately, this type of ship has relatively few commercial applications, so if the military wants many of them in time of crisis it must buy most of what it needs.

Lighter-Aboard-Ship (LASH)

LASH can load and unload itself using the shallow draft barges it carries. A port is a convenience! Unfortunately, once again, this type of ship has relatively few commercial applications so if the military wants many in time of crisis it must buy most of what it needs.

Desert Shield Strategic Airlift

Cargo (Tons)

- C-5 48.2 %
- Commercial 20.1 %
- KC-10 3.4 %
- C-141 29.3 %

Passengers

- C-5 23.4 %
- Commercial 60.0 %
- C-141 16.4 %
- KC-10 .2 %

PLANNING THE ATTACK
BLUEPRINT FOR VICTORY

Even while the forces of the Coalition were still being assembled, planning for the Desert Storm offensive had begun. The offensive would be carried out in two phases: a massive, sustained aerial bombardment followed by a brief, shatteringly violent ground offensive aimed at the complete destruction of Iraqi forces deployed in the Kuwaiti Theater of Operations.

Lieutenant General Charles Horner, the air commander of Desert Shield, had already assembled a brilliant planning staff, including Colonel John A. Warden III (more widely known for his book *The Air Campaign: Planning for Combat*). He now set to work generating a campaign plan that would leave the Iraqi forces prostrate.

At the same time, the broad out-

lines of the ground campaign were sketched. Clearly, Saddam expected a frontal assault on Kuwait and had massed the majority of his forces there. These troops were backed by a layer of regular army armored and mechanized divisions, and then the whole structure was backed by the Republican Guard Forces Command.

This force of seven divisions was the key to the campaign in several respects. Not only was it the most capable of the combat forces at the disposal of the Iraqis, it was also a force of tremendous political significance. Saddam's close association with the Republican Guard, and its mission of maintaining Saddam in power, made it an important objective in and of itself.

In any campaign it is critical to identify the enemy's center of gravity and direct your maximum effort at that point. Having identified the Guard as the Iraqi center of gravity, the mass of the Coalition's heavy mechanized forces were tasked with bypassing the main Iraqi defenses and striking directly at the Guard.

To carry this out, three principal considerations had to be addressed: politics, security, and logistics.

POLITICS

In order to bypass the main Iraqi defenses, it would be necessary to swing wide into Iraqi territory. While the United States and its European allies (France and the United Kingdom) were primed for operations inside Iraqi territory, divided popular opinion in the Islamic countries of the Coalition made it more difficult to use their forces in this way. (In fact, most of these

---

WHO'S WHO: THE US FORCES

General Norman Schwarzkopf, USA: Colorful and gifted commander of US Central Command. Has been compared to Patton; future US generals will be compared to him. Often called "Stormin' Norman" by the troops, but prefers his family's nickname for him, "The Bear."

General Calvin Waller, USA: Schwarzkopf's deputy commander. Commanded 3rd Army during the offensive in place of Lt. Gen. Yeosock.

Lieutenant General John Yeosock, USA: Hard working non-West Point commander of 3rd Army. Known as a determined and intelligent officer. Fell ill one week before the ground war started, but left 3rd Army well prepared for a tremendous victory.

Lieutenant General Charles Horner, USAF: Commander of the joint air forces of Central Command. To ensure close cooperation with ground forces at every level, Horner roomed with Yeosock in Saudi Arabia.

Vice Admiral Stanley Arthur, USN: Commander of US 7th Fleet and coordinated activities of 120 US and 50 Allied vessels. Navy flyer in Vietnam with 500+ missions and Distinguished Flying Cross.

Lieutenant General Walter Boomer, USMC: Commander of all Marine forces in the gulf. "We made a lot of stupid mistakes in Vietnam, mistakes we're not going to repeat here."

Major General Robert Johnston, USMC: Chief of staff, US Central Command. Born and raised in Scotland, he emigrated to the United States at 18 and joined the US Marine Corps. Moved the 700-person staff from Florida to Saudi Arabia without a hitch. Coordinates the work of a talented multiservice staff nicknamed "The Jedi Knights."

Major General William Pagonis, USA: Operation Desert Storm's brilliant chief logistician. Said another US general, "I think it will probably go down in history as one of the most amazing logistical moves there's ever been. We moved a whole corps of over 100,000 people over 300 miles, mostly along one road, the Tap Line Road, and we did that in 16 days, with all the combat service support, all the logistics, all the ammunition."

governments had publicly assured their populations that their troops would not enter Iraqi territory.) Consequently, it was necessary to use the US, British, and French as a flanking force, and the Coalition troops for the drive against Kuwait.

It would not do, however, to stick the non-European members of the Coalition with the dirty job of pounding through the toughest part of the line while the US had the "easy" job of a flank run. Consequently, the US Marines were deployed in corps strength to make the toughest of the line-breaching attacks, and be poised to cooperate with any possible amphibious attack along the coast.

SECURITY

Saddam was obligingly packing troops into Kuwait, which would simply make the prisoner haul that much bigger when the encirclement came. He had to be encouraged to continue doing so, however, and so the intent of the Allied plan had to be disguised. To that end, all US forces were deployed south of Kuwait until the air offensive was well under way. Once the Iraqi capability to conduct air reconnaissance was crippled, the heavy forces could begin moving west to their assembly areas, but not before.

Continuous aggressive patrolling by Marines, Joint Arab Forces, and eventually the 1st Cavalry Division (armored) against the Kuwaiti border maintained the illusion of the major blow falling there. The Marine and 1st Cavalry attacks were so convincing that the Iraqis thought the offensive had started as much as 24 hours before it actually jumped off.

LOGISTICS

Modern heavy forces consume staggering amounts of supply. To meet this need, large supply dumps would be established well to the west along the Iraqi border. Once the war started,

most truck assets would be tied up supplying the forward troops, which meant the supply dumps would be eaten down quickly, so all of the supplies needed for the campaign would have to dumped in advance. To be safe, provisions were made for a six-week offensive.

Security intervened at this point. Dumping operations could not begin before the air campaign started, as Iraqi recon aircraft flying along the border would see the activity and determine its purpose. Therefore the movement of supplies west had to wait until the air campaign was under way

GULF WAR
F A C T B O O K
The War

and the Iraqis had been blinded. This had to be done along the same road, and at the same time, as the movement west of the heavy divisions, an extraordinarily difficult undertaking.

WHO'S WHO: THE IRAQI FORCES

Staff-Marshal Saddam Hussein: Supreme commander of all Iraqi forces. Personally planned the Khafji attacks, and micro-managed the deployment of troops in the Kuwaiti Theater of Operations. No prior military service, even as an enlisted man.

General Adnan Khairallah: Saddam's brother-in-law. Led the Republican Guard in the closing stages of the Iran-Iraq War in a series of smashing victories on the southern front. After the war became defense minister. Talented, practical, and too popular for his own good. Killed in helicopter "accident," May 1989. Replaced by *General Abdel Jabbar Shanshal*, who advised against the war. Sacked in December of 1990 and replaced by *General Saadi Tb'ma Abbas*, a political yes-man.

General Nizar Abdel Karim al-Khazraji: Career officer with a brilliant combat and staff record. Chief of staff at the end of the Iran-Iraq War and during the invasion of Kuwait. Sacked and replaced by *General Hussein al-Takriti*, a political hack from Saddam's hometown.

Lieutenant General Maher Abdel Rashid: Led both the 2nd and 3rd Corps to victory by the end of the Iran-Iraq War. A gifted commander who became a national hero during the war, and whose daughter married Saddam's youngest son. Objected to preferential treatment given to the Republican Guard; relieved of command in the summer of 1988, and reportedly now under surveillance.

General Dhaffer Abdel Rashid: Cousin of Lt. General Maher Abdel Rashid. Experienced and successful field commander. Killed in helicopter "accident" in early 1988.

General Abdel Aziz Ibrahim al-Hadithi: Experienced and successful field commander. Killed in helicopter "accident" some time in 1988.

General Salman Shuja: Experienced and successful field commander. Killed in helicopter "accident."

Lieutenant General Saleh Abboud: Commander of Iraqi 3rd Corps during the Khafji attacks and the following Coalition offensive. Unknown political general who held no important commands during the Iran-Iraq War.

THE AIR CAMPAIGN

The first five and a half weeks of Desert Storm were described as "the air war," the final 100 hours, "the ground war." This implies there were two separate wars, both largely independent. Historians often speak this way also, either through parochialism or overspecialization. It ain't so. Moreso than most wars, air, sea, land, and even diplomacy were integrated into one unified campaign plan. If we speak of an air campaign we are merely referring to the middle phase of a war that started on August 2 with the Iraqi invasion of Kuwait and ended with the virtual destruction of all Iraqi forces in the Kuwaiti area of operations.

SMART PEOPLE

Much of the publicity during Operation Desert Storm has gone to smart weapons. While these weapons undoubtedly saved countless lives—of both Coalition soldiers and Iraqi civilians—they do not come close to explaining the Coalition's lopsided victory. After all, the Iraqi Air Force had smart weapons, too. Decisions made by smart people determined how those smart weapons would be used—and which side would get to use them.

THE PLAN

A lesson from Vietnam would ensure the air campaign plan would be focused. During Vietnam there were five allied air forces that more or less did their thing, the South Vietnamese Air Force, the US Air Force, aircraft of the US Navy, air-craft of the US Marine Corps, and aircraft of the Strategic Air Command. General Schwarzkopf, a student of military history in general and in the lessons of Vietnam in particular, knew the lost opportunities this lack of unifying direction had cost and made it clear from the start there would be one air boss and it would be US Air Force Lieutenant General Charles Horner.

Horner brought together a small planning team with representatives of each service. The team included not only "airplane drivers," but logisticians and intelligence specialists. Other Coalition air forces became full partners in building the plan. The plan was much more than a target list. The sequence in which targets were attacked was closely scrutinized both for possible impact on friendly losses and overall war objectives and exploited Coalition capabilities.

Schwarzkopf loved it.

IN A NUTSHELL

The plan called for air power to be used in each major area of application throughout the campaign, and for the level of effort in each area to shift as the campaign progressed.

- The early weight of effort went to gaining control of the air, with some aircraft hitting the most important strategic targets and the B-52s hitting the Republican Guard.
- As air superiority was achieved, more weight would be given to strategic targets, interdiction, and to hitting the Iraqi Army.
- Finally, when air supremacy was achieved and the most strategic targets hit, most effort would go to cutting off the Iraqi Army in the Kuwaiti Theater of Operations throughout interdiction and killing it by direct attack from the air.

THE FIRST MINUTES

One of the dangers of trying to write the history of events which occurred so recently is that the conflicting versions have yet to be sorted out. In this case, though, the conflicting claims for the "first shot" serve to illustrate the joint nature of the air campaign. According to one version, the first act of hostilities was when US Army special forces teams put adjacent Iraqi radars off the air so Coalition aircraft could proceed undetected through the gap. In another, all navy cruise missiles were timed to reach their targets at the same time, creating the confusion that allowed all the manned aircraft to penetrate. In yet another version, the first shot was the bomb dropped by an F-117A on the headquarters of the Iraqi Air Force. Finally, there was one report that the first shots fired were from two marine helicopters putting an Iraqi electronic listening post out of action. Whatever the truth, it is clear from the conflicting claims that the air campaign was much more than an air force effort.

THE FIRST WAVE

Whatever the exact sequence, the first wave followed this general pattern. Surprise and stealth were exploited to hit heavily defended, high-value targets first. When stealthy attacks (by whatever means) had put out the eyes of the Iraqi integrated air defense system and disrupted its communications, the rest of the attacking aircraft entered Iraqi airspace.

High-priority targets that first night included those that would minimize Coalition casualties during the remainder of the operation. Fixed Scud sites and mobile launchers that could be found were a high priority.

One of the highest priorities was shooting down the Iraqi Air Force. This Royal Air Force (RAF) Tornados did with dispatch. The Iraqi's also knew the importance of their air bases and defended them heavily. During just the first week, the RAF suffered the highest percentage losses of any aircraft for the entire war.

Hitting Iraqi SAMs hard that first night was also crucial. With the SAMs ineffective, Coalition aircraft could fly above the effective range of the AAA.

By the time the aircraft were returning from the first wave it was clear something historic had occurred. *No* losses had occurred during the first hours of the attack! Even as some aircraft were lost later in the day, the loss rate would have once been considered acceptable for a peacetime training exercise.

Sometimes air power can achieve political objectives directly. It seemed an objective of several Coalition partners to remove the threat of Iraqi nuclear, chemical and biological weapons. These sites were hit early and hard.

THE FRUSTRATIONS OF SCUD HUNTING

Despite miraculously low losses and high initial success, the air campaign did encounter two unexpected difficulties.

One was the difficulty in tracking down and killing the mobile Scud launchers. A low prewar estimate of the Iraqi inventory of launchers and Iraqi use of deception, camouflage, and hardening kept hunting Scuds a challenge to the end of Desert Storm. It proved such a drain on sorties that it appears to have delayed the start of the ground offensive by several days.

The other surprise was that the Iraqi Air Force did not cooperate and "come up" so the Coalition could shoot it down. Actually, the inaction of the Iraqi Air Force would not have been a surprise to anyone who had studied it. For many years American airmen have believed they should launch as many sorties each day as possible. Iraqi doctrine has been that an air force is an important reserve to be used when it can achieve decisive results and conserved when it cannot. Anyway, Iraq's best aircraft were in shelters that were built to withstand penetration by any conventional weapon.

When the Coalition started dropping the new, laser-guided I-2000 bombs, it was the Iraqis' turn to be surprised. The shelter-busting started on January 25 and the flights to Iran began the next day. Whether or not the departure of much of the best of the Iraqi Air Force was a sign of panic or a deliberate plan to tie up a portion of the Coalition's air power "just in case" the aircraft returned, it had that effect.

THE SHIFT TO INTERDICTION

Smart weapons have quite correctly received great credit for the effectiveness of an interdiction campaign that reduced entire divisions to drinking rain water and

eating grass, but it is hardly the entire story. The success of the Coalition air forces' interdiction efforts began with the success of the Coalition navies' enforcement of the UN embargo. The less ammunition and spare parts coming into Iraq, the more any destroyed during interdiction would be missed.

In a similar way, strategic attacks on Iraqi ammunition plants also increased the impact of interdiction.

Finally, the need to transport even water to the Iraqi troops, the need to probe Coalition lines for intelligence, and to respond to Coalition probes created demands on Iraqi supply lines that the interdiction effort made sure could not be met.

PREPARING THE BATTLEFIELD

No one expected the collapse of the Iraqi front-line units, at least not until after it happened. None of the satellites, reconnaissance aircraft, or electronic warfare platforms could see inside the heart of the Iraqi soldier. Asked to die for a cause few believed in, he had seen many friends killed but he had probably not seen any attacking aircraft shot down. With little support from the rear and no opportunity to fight back, in hindsight the reasons he stopped fighting seem clear. Air power has a physical and a psychological effect: You can take pictures of the physical effects, but the psychological effects can only be seen by their results.

REHEARSAL
THE BATTLE OF KHAFJI

Once the air offensive began, the Iraqi Air Force was quickly put out of action: either destroyed, forced to flee to Iran, or pinned down in its shelters. This blinded the Iraqi high command, and made it difficult for it to gain adequate information about Allied strength and deployments.

Early patrolling activity was largely unsuccessful. Probably in response to this, the Iraqis decided to launch a series of larger attacks. These may have been intended as large reconnaissance in force missions, or they may have been intended to drive back the Allied front lines and overrun artillery positions which had been shelling the Iraqis. In either case, the decision resulted in a series of battles over the course of several days, the most famous of which was at Khafji.

In order to carry out these attacks, mechanized forces from the second defensive echelon were brought forward to reinforce the organic tank and special forces battalions of the front-line Iraqi infantry divisions. Total forces committed amounted to at least four battalions of mechanized infantry and four battalions of tanks.

1. THE ELBOW
2300 Hours, 29 January 1991

The border between Kuwait and Saudi Arabia travels due west from the shores of the Persian Gulf for about 40 miles, then abruptly turns northwest. There are a series of low gravel hills which run from northwest to southeast along the border and then further south, and the high ground here offers several good vantage points for observing activity inside Kuwait.

The high ground near this "elbow" was patrolled by troops of the 3rd Marine Regiment, 1st Marine Division, usually in HMMWV soft-skinned vehicles or LAV-25 infantry fighting vehicles. In the late evening of January 29, Marine forces in the vicinity of Point 220 identified a hostile mechanized column approaching from the northeast. The force was a combined arms task force consisting of a battalion of mechanized infantry reinforced with about 20 tanks.

The Marines immediately called for artillery support, and brought the Iraqi column under direct fire. At first the battle was fought by the light of flares, but eventually the sun rose and the fight continued.

2. KHAFJI SEIZED
2330 Hours, 29 January 1991

Slightly after the first attack had been launched, an Iraqi mechanized infantry battalion mounted in Chinese Type 63 APCs, reinforced with a company of T-55 tanks and a platoon of ERC-90 armored cars, launched an attack south along the coast road toward Khafji. Khafji, with a pre-war population of 85,000, was one of the larger Saudi towns, but it had been attacked by Iraqi artillery fire shortly after the start of hostilities and its inhabitants had been evacuated farther south. As a result, on January 29, it was a ghost town. The defensive line north of it consisted only of a few scattered outposts of the Saudi 5th Airborne Battalion.

At about 2230 hours the advanced guard of the Iraqi battalion, with one mechanized company, a platoon of tanks, and a few armored cars, slammed through the lightly held roadblocks and took Khafji on the run. By the early hours of January 30 the rest of the reinforced Iraqi battalion had joined the advanced guard, although the arrival of these reinforcements apparently escaped the notice of the Saudis.

Khafji was not completely deserted, however. There were two six-man recon patrols of the 1st Marine Division in the city at the time of the Iraqi attack. Caught by surprise, the Marines played a deadly game of cat-and-mouse with the Iraqis for the next 36 hours, avoiding detection and calling in artillery strikes by radio.

3. THE PUNCH
UP THE MIDDLE
1000 Hours, 30 January 1991

To the north of Khafji, the Iraqis still held one battalion each of mechanized infantry and tanks in reserve. Instead of reinforcing their success at Khafji, however, at 1000 hours they launched a separate attack nearly 15 miles inland. The attack column was led by tanks with their turrets reversed, the signal for surrender described in Coalition PsyOps leaflets distributed over the Iraqi lines for the past week. As a result, the column got into the positions of the Allied covering force before suffering losses.

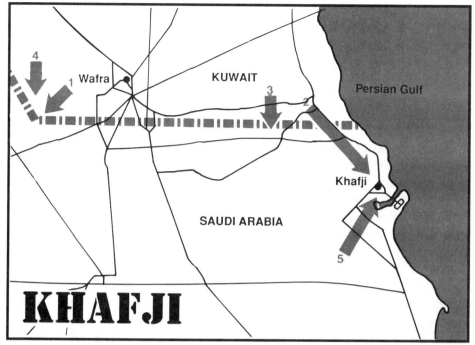

KHAFJI

The troops holding the line here were Saudi National Guardsmen of the King Faisal Brigade and a Qatari mechanized battalion reinforced by a company of AMX-30 tanks. The Saudis and Qataris opened fire and called for artillery and air support. An intense, confused battle followed, but the Iraqis were forced to withdraw in the early afternoon after sustaining heavy losses. Two of the Iraqi tanks were knocked out by the Qatari tankers.

4. THE ELBOW—SECOND WAVE
0600 Hours, 30 January 1991

Although their earlier attack in the west had been stopped by the Marines, the Iraqis still had two uncommitted battalions available, one each of tanks and infantry. In the early morning hours of the 30th they launched them south in an attempt to break through the Marine defensive positions. Because of the greater strength of the attack it apparently drove to within 25 meters of the forward Marine positions.

At first light, A-10 Army ground attack aircraft joined the Marine

AH-1 Cobra gunships and Harriers in hitting the advancing tanks. Pounded by artillery and air-launched antitank missiles, as well as the stubborn Marine ground defenders, the Iraqis lost 12 more tanks, and a large number of APCs. However, in the heat of battle a US attack aircraft mistook the Marines' eight-wheeled LAV-25s for Soviet-built BTR-60 APCs and destroyed two of them. Twelve Marines were killed in this first "friendly fire" incident of the war.

At 0900, after more than nine hours of what one Marine officer described as "hellacious combat" the Iraqis broke off the action and retreated, having lost 24 tanks, over a dozen APCs, and well over a 100 casualties.

5. COUNTERATTACK
Wednesday and Thursday, 30-31 January 1991

The ease with which Khafji had fallen was a source of some embarrassment to the Saudis. The Saudis requested that the US Marines, who were deployed in a backstop position, leave the recapture of Khafji to

the Saudis.

A battalion of Saudi National Guard mechanized infantry moved up from reserve positions and launched a hasty counterattack on the city on the morning of the 30th. Thinking it was held only by a company, the volume of fire came as a surprise and pushed the counterattack force back. Several additional attacks were launched throughout the morning, eventually reinforced by a company of Saudi M60 tanks. Once the Saudis and Qataris to the west were freed up by the retreat of the central Iraqi column, they were added to the attack, but the Iraqis managed to hold. At about this time, however, most of the Iraqi tank battalion broke out of Khafji and retreated north. Many of these tanks were subsequently knocked out by ground attack aircraft.

In the late evening, the Saudis and Qataris finally broke into Khafji and secured the center of the town, although the sheer size of the built-up area meant that the mopping up part of the operation would last for more than an additional day. The Marine recon teams were rescued.

The final cost of the counterattack to the Saudis was 18 dead, 29 wounded, and four missing, with two tanks and six other AFVs put out of action. The Iraqis lost an entire infantry battalion, with 30 dead and 450 prisoners. All of the battalion's APCs were disabled, along with about a dozen tanks.

(top right box)

GULF WAR
FACT BOOK
The War

MARINES & THE JOINT ARAB COMMAND
CRACKING THE SADDAM LINE

The overall plan of attack required that the Coalition troops arrayed along the Kuwaiti border not only attack, but that they do so vigorously enough to pull the Iraqi mobile reserves south farther into the bag. As a prelude to the actual offensive, the 1st Cavalry Division and the 1st Marine Expeditionary Force launched a series of operations against Iraqi forces along the border. These provoked only a feeble and uncoordinated response. This was an early indication that the Iraqi Army had very little fight left in it.

SUNDAY

(See map on page 104.) At 0400 hours on February 24, the first blows of the offensive were struck. These consisted of a two-division attack by the 1st Marine Expeditionary Force and a breaching operation by the Joint Forces Command–East. These troops were as far away from the actual thrust of the main attack as possible.

The assaults went in briskly, and immediately began generating large numbers of enemy prisoners of war (EPWs). Even though the defenses were thick and stepped well back from the border, Iraqi resistance was startlingly brief. Three Iraqi divisions (7th, 14th, and 29th) disintegrated as the two Marine divisions executed a textbook break-in operation. Farther west the Joint Forces Command troops also made progress against the Iraqi 18th Infantry Division.

Given the mounting evidence of a general collapse, Central Command moved forward the date of the general offensive, and all other units launched in the afternoon of February 24. (See map on page 102.)

To the north of the Marines, the first unit through the sand berm was the Kuwait 35th "Al-Shahid" (Martyrs) Armored Brigade. With Soviet-style vehicles (M-84 tanks and BMP-2 infantry fighting vehicles), air recognition was a major concern, and every vehicle had a large orange recognition panel on the engine deck. They were followed by he RSLF 20th Mechanized Brigade which, with the Kuwaitis, formed Task Force Muthana. Their objective was Kuwait City.

Protecting the left flank of TF Muthana was the Saudi 9th Armored Division, and farther west the Egyptian II Corps launched both divisions into the positions of the Iraqi 26th Infantry Division. They lost several tanks early on to mines, but kept advancing and soon began taking prisoners in large numbers.

MONDAY

(See the map on page 103.) Throughout February 25, the Coalition forces struggled to break free of the multiple lines of obstacles and minefields, as well as the swarms of prisoners. The roads were choked with surrendering Iraqis, which slowed the supply vehicles and follow-up troops trying to push forward.

An additional problem that surfaced had to do with traffic control. While the Egyptians and Syrians had considerable experience in moving large formations of troops in combat, as did the Marines, the other Joint Forces had effectively none.

As the day progressed, the Egyptians finished mopping up the Iraqi 26th Division and broke free into the open. By nightfall they had begun moving east toward Kuwait City, with the Syrians on their right.

While Marine columns broke free and began rolling north, Saudi and Kuwaiti columns remained snarled in huge traffic jams. The 2nd Marine Division extended its right flank to link up with the Joint Forces Command–East, thus isolating the remnants of the Iraqi 8th Infantry Division. The drive north brought the Marines, and the attached "Tiger" brigade into contact with the Iraqi 5th Mechanized Division (with about 150 T-62 tanks), which they quickly shot to pieces.

TUESDAY

Throughout the day the Coalition forces closed in on Kuwait City, collecting swarms of prisoners, and slowed more by mines and traffic delays than enemy resistance. By midday, the Iraqi III Corps, which controlled the 10 infantry divisions deployed along the Kuwaiti border, had ceased to exist. IV Corps was disintegrating while the divisions of VIII Tank Corps were holding their ground, if only temporarily.

At Kuwait International Airport, advancing US Marines encountered the Iraqi 3rd Armored Division with at least some semblance of order remaining. After several scattered tank duels, the Marines isolated the airport by nightfall and prepared to launch a morning attack.

It was also at about this time that elements of the 2nd Marine Expeditionary Force were landed behind friendly lines to reinforce the drive north. This force was the 5th Marine Expeditionary Brigade (reinforced), and it came under control of the 2nd Marine Division upon landing.

The Marines could have entered Kuwait City on Tuesday, but the decision had been made to leave the liberation of the city to Task Force Muthana, spearheaded by the Kuwaiti 35th Brigade. Since the 35th had offered a spirited resistance to the invasion six months earlier and then withdrawn in fair order, there was a compelling justice to this. Task Force Muthana had been making

slow ground, though, as it plowed its way through the remnants of three Iraqi infantry divisions (16th, 21st, and 36th).

Fortunately, there was little urgency in the operation at this stage. The 11th Iraqi Division in Kuwait City was surrendering to the Kuwaiti resistance in the thousands, and had effectively disappeared as a formation.

WEDNESDAY AND BEYOND

At 0900 hours on February 27, just 77 hours after the start of the offensive, the Kuwaiti 35th Brigade entered Kuwait City, followed closely by the RSLF 20th Brigade and US Special Forces troops. Scenes in the streets of the city were reminiscent of the arrival of the French 2nd Armored Division in Paris in 1944. And as with Paris, the combat troops had been preceded into Kuwait City by newsmen. In Paris it had been Ernest Hemingway; in Kuwait City it was CBS reporter Bob McKeown and his crew. "We drove into the city with no problem whatsoever," he said.

At first light, the Marines moved into the Kuwait International Airport area and began finishing off the Iraqi 3rd Armored Division. By 0900 over a hundred more Iraqi tanks were burning and the division was finished. The Marines began moving into the southern outskirts of Kuwait City.

All that remained in Kuwait of an Iraqi garrison of 22 divisions in three large corps were mobs of fugitives heading north, being pounded to pieces on the roads by Coalition attack aircraft. For the last 24 hours of the war the troops in the south were mostly preoccupied with mopping up small pockets of Iraqi soldiers, most of whom were anxious to surrender.

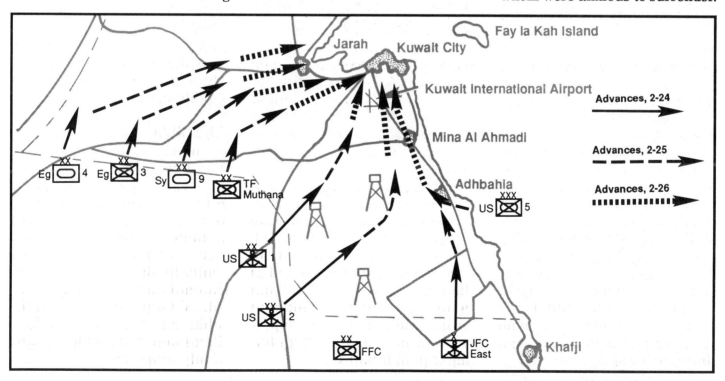

XVIII AIRBORNE CORPS CLOSES THE GATE
THE WIDE SWEEP

The mission of 3rd Army was not only to eject Iraq from Kuwait, but also to establish the military preconditions for a lasting peace. For a variety of reasons, Iraq's enormous military capability was seen to be a destabilizing influence in the region, and was a principal target of Desert Storm.

The mission plan called for the Marines and Joint Forces Command to pin the Iraqis in place while VII Corps executed a wide outflanking move to the west. XVIII Airborne Corps played a vital role in the operation by cutting off all escape and reinforcement routes to the KTO and by covering the exposed rear echelons of VII Corps when it turned east to face the Republican Guard.

In order to carry out this dual encirclement/security mission, XVIII Airborne Corps consisted of as diverse a collection of troops as fought on the Coalition side. The four divisions of the corps included a light armored division, a heavy mechanized division, an airmobile division, and an airborne division operating primarily in the light motorized role.

On the far inland flank, the French Daguet Division (6th Light Armored Division, heavily reinforced), with a truck-mounted brigade of the US 82nd Airborne Division attached, was responsible for driving northeast and seizing the key road junctions in the area between Rafha and As Samawah on the Euphrates River.

In the middle of the corps, the 101st Airmobile Division, again with elements of the 82nd Airborne attached, was to make the big move in the center. It would make an airmobile assault on the air base at An Nasiriyah, severing the retreat route of the Republican Guard up the Euphrates River valley. Since An Nasiriyah was too far to make in one jump, the division would first seize the abandoned airfield at Al Ubayyid and establish a forward logistical base there, stocked by heavy helicopters. The division would then make the second move forward to the Euphrates.

On the right, the 24th Infantry Division (Mechanized), with the 3rd Armored Cavalry Regiment attached, would drive wide to the west of VII Corps and hook in on the Guard from the northeast. It would aim at Jalibah, and then turn east, supported by the Apache gunships of the 101st, which would by then be established at Nasiriyah. Its path would be prepared by extensive strategic recon missions conducted on the ground by 5th Special Forces Group.

It was an audacious plan, but one well-tailored to the unique capabilities of each of the corps' component units.

SUNDAY

(See map on page 102.) Given the nature of the corps' mission, there was little chance of ground contact on the first day; there just weren't that many Iraqi troops up close to the border on this flank. The 24th on the right and the Daguet Division on the left moved across the border in the afternoon. The 24th moved west of the main Iraqi troop concentrations, looking for open roads rather than a fight. The Daguet Division's mission, on the other hand, required that it seek out the Iraqi troops to the west, and its motorized patrols fanned out in search of the enemy.

The only solid contact on the first day came in the center when the lead brigade of the 101st dropped in unannounced at Al Ubayyid and scooped up 500 prisoners from the Iraqi 26th Infantry Division.

The initial lift involved a force of 2000 ground troops, 50 light vehicles, towed artillery pieces, and supplies—all lifted by 300 transport helicopters and escorting gunships, the largest helicopter assault in military history. Meanwhile an additional brigade moved overland on wheels. With the advanced guard on the ground, they quickly cleared a 60-square-mile divisional encampment, dubbed "Cobra Base," and prepared before the next leg of the trip.

MONDAY

(See map on page 103.) While deteriorating weather bedeviled the 101st's attempts to build up supplies forward by helicopter, the Daguet Division ran roughshod over the Iraqi 45th Infantry Division in the west, and sent light motorized patrols racing north along the muddy roads. Within 36 hours of the initiation of the ground offensive, the French and their attached US Airborne troopers had seized every objective and had taken over 3000 prisoners.

On the right flank, the 24th Mech was making good time to the north with only light contact with the enemy. The ease with which the division and its attached armored cavalry regiment were advancing should not obscure the importance of their mission. If the

Republican Guard dug in and fought against the VII Corps, the 24th Division would decisively tip the balance in the Coalition's favor.

Why? Because the 24th had achieved every cavalryman's dream: It had disappeared from the enemy's maps and was running at full speed deep into his rear areas. When it reappeared, it would be with total surprise and shattering force.

TUESDAY

While the French established an active patrolling program on the left flank and pushed patrols north toward As Samawah and Najuf, the 101st made the next leg of its jump and hit An Nasiriyah, scattering the reservists of the Iraqi 49th Infantry Division. The division was the first Coalition unit to reach the Euphrates River, and cut the retreat route of the Iraqi forces farther east.

Cobra Base was in full operation now, ferrying in supplies, maintaining aircraft, and serving as a staging point for troops being ferried north to the Euphrates valley. Farther east, the 24th Mech was closing on Jalibah and beginning to contact the Iraqi forces west of Basra.

WEDNESDAY AND BEYOND

The French continued patrolling, but there was no sign of enemy reinforcements moving south to break the encirclement. As with the other fronts, there was a notable lack of coherent Iraqi response to the offensive, for a variety of reasons.

First, there was a lack of direction and leadership from above. Saddam had micromanaged the battle prior to this; now he decided to take an inspection trip to the I Corps in Kurdistan. In all likelihood, the Iraqi general staff in Baghdad received almost no useful information to make operational decisions with, and probably lacked the talent or will to do so in any event.

Second, the ability of commanders to get operational instructions quickly and securely to their troops had been degraded virtually to nil. If Baghdad or Basra had had a good view of the battle and had been able to formulate a course of action to deal with it, they would have found it nearly impossible to communicate it to the troops.

Third, the troops were finished, especially the front-line troops. Their capacity for offensive action was long gone, and their ability to resist was nearly so as well. That is not to say that they did not fight; many of them did. If the campaign had been a slow, cautious one, attacking casualties would have been high. Even exhausted troops can take considerable pressure if it is applied gradually.

But 3rd Army did not apply the pressure gradually. When an Iraqi division was attacked, it was attacked suddenly, violently, and with overwhelming force. And in those circumstances, the divisions just collapsed, one after another.

On the left, the 24th Mech and its attached troops began encountering infantry and armor east in the vicinity of Jalibah. These were better troops than had been encountered near the border, probably from the "Al Faw" Division of the Republican Guard. But while the fight was more spirited, it was ultimately just as one-sided.

Further south, the "Hammurabi" Armored Division was fighting a desperate delaying action to let the bulk of the Guard escape. The only remaining escape route was north along the Tigris River valley by a narrow road which crosses several bridges at major waterways. These bridges had been hammered from the air for over a week, though, and now the last ones left standing were blown by special forces teams. The Republican Guards were trapped.

Backed up by the division's own attack helicopter battalion and additional aviation assets from the 101st Air Assault, the 24th Mech pressed forward and turned the area southwest of Basra into a vast killing ground. Linked in with the VII Corps to the south, the 24th now pushed and slashed at the Iraqis until the whole army just seemed to melt away, leaving behind a landscape littered with discarded equipment and broken, burning armored vehicles.

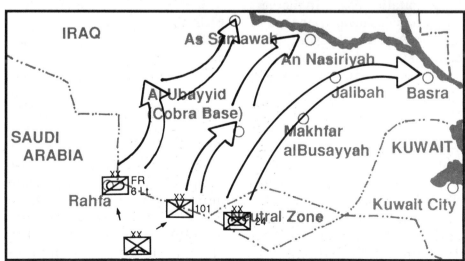

VII CORPS DELIVERS THE KNOCKOUT PUNCH
COUP DE GRACE

With Iraqi attention riveted on southern Kuwait and XVIII Airborne Corps swinging wide to the west to cut off all avenues of escape up the Euphrates River valley, VII Corps prepared to launch a phalanx of over 2000 armored fighting vehicles through the thin screen in the Neutral Zone and directly at the Republic Guard.

SUNDAY

(See map on page 102.) Although the corps was scheduled to jump off after dark on the night of February 24-25, the excellent progress of the attacks to the east caused the corps to move up its attack date to the early afternoon. The corps was deployed to break through along a three-division frontage. These three divisions were the US 1st Infantry (Mechanized), US 1st Armored, and US 3rd Armored Divisions (from east to west). Once the line was breached, the second echelon would exploit through and lead the exploitation north. In the west this second echelon consisted of the 2nd Armored Cavalry Regiment. In the east, however, there were several divisions deployed along the "seam" between Iraq and Kuwait, and a heavier follow-up force was necessary: 1st British Armoured Division.

As soon as the attack was launched, VII Corps knew it had a clean breakthrough, as the experience farther south was repeated. 1st Infantry Division (Mechanized) drove right through the Iraqi 27th Infantry Division, overran what little artillery had escaped the air bombardment, and consolidated on its objective hours ahead of schedule. 1st British Armoured Division passed through its position and leapfrogged on ahead.

Farther west the 1st Armored Division hit the seam between the Iraqi 48th and 25th Divisions and bowled through both of them, encountering no effective resistance on the ground. The Iraqi 31st Infantry, deployed as a second defensive echelon to the rear, was overrun and destroyed nearly as quickly. On the left flank, 3rd Armored made even better time, having turned the corner around the left flank of the Iraqi line.

2nd Armored Cavalry Regiment passed through the armor and broke out into open spaces beyond. There was nothing between it and the Republican Guard but open sand. It traced 45 miles into Iraq before being reined in to give the armored divisions a chance to catch up.

MONDAY

(See map on page 103.) On the corps' right flank, the 1st Infantry (Mechanized) and 1st British Armoured Divisions continued to chew up the divisions along the western rim of the Wadi al Batin. By day's end they had chewed up the 12th Armored and 47th Infantry divisions, and were turning east to cut off any units trying to retreat west from Kuwait.

To their left, the 2nd Armored Cavalry Regiment led the drive forward by 1st and 3rd Armored all day, slowed up more by the deteriorating weather than by enemy resistance. During the course of the day, the corps overran and rounded up scattered elements of the Iraqi 26th Infantry Division. By nightfall, the left flank of the corps had secured the vital crossroads at Makhfar al Busayyah. From now on the corps would be advancing to the east instead of north.

TUESDAY

For the first time, VII Corps came in contact with heavy elements of the Republican Guard. The entire corps was now completing the pivot and was deployed along a line from south to north instead of east to west. The whole line now ground forward, an irresistible mincing machine that shredded everything in its path.

By day's end a reserve armored division attached to the Republican Guard, as well as the Guard's own 3rd "Tawakalna" Mechanized Division had been destroyed. The 2nd "Medina" Armored Division was also in retreat, and was probably at no more than half strength.

24th Mechanized Division (from XVIII Airborne Corps) was positioned to the north, having closed the gap to the Euphrates, and all escape routes were plugged. It was already in contact with elements of the Republican Guard, probably the 4th "Al Faw" Motorized Division.

By late in the day, Coalition intelligence estimated that 21 of the 42 Iraqi divisions in the KTO were no longer combat effective. Many of the rest were in full retreat.

WEDNESDAY AND BEYOND

As the Iraqi Army streamed north, the premier division of the Republican Guard, the 1st "Hammurabi," prepared to fight a stubborn delaying action to gain time for the withdrawal of the rest of the corps.

Visibility was virtually nil, due both to weather and the smoke from hundreds of burning well heads in Kuwait, and this was one of the factors that proved the undoing of the "Hammurabi" Division.

In a day-long confused brawl with the 1st and 3rd Armored Divisions, the Guard division was hammered to pieces, at a cost of only one or two damaged M1A1s. As poor as the visibility was, the M1A1 and Bradley crews fought

using their thermal sights, which cut through the rain and smoke to give good enough target images to engage and hit.

US tanks repeatedly drove into Iraqi tank ambushes and got off the first shot, because they could see the hidden Iraqi vehicles before the Iraqis could detect the US vehicles moving in the open. In most duels the US fired the only shots, and surviving Iraqi tank crews later reported that they seldom were able to tell where the hostile fire was coming from.

By Wednesday, Coalition intelligence estimated that 27 divisions had been knocked out of the war, leaving only 15 combat-effective divisions in the rapidly shrinking pocket south of Basra. These included an armored division (probably the 17th), perhaps half of the 2nd "Medina" Armored Division, and three other divisions of the Republican Guard. The 8th Special Forces Division was certainly among these, and the other two may have been the 6th "Nebuchadnezzar" and 7th "Adnan" Motorized Infantry Divisions.

By the end of hostilities, every division in the Guard, as well as every regular division in the Kuwaiti Theater of Operations, had been rendered combat ineffective. Scattered groups of infantry and tank crews escaped on foot, but the Iraqi Army in the KTO had been completely smashed as an instrument of war.

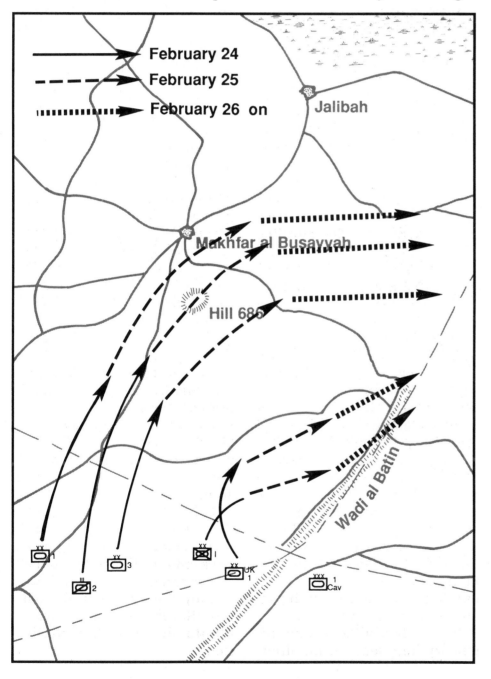

February 24
February 25
February 26 on
Jalibah
Makhfar al Busayyah
Hill 686
Wadi al Batin

SPECIAL OPERATIONS
MODERN COMMANDOS

The United States entered the conflict in the Persian Gulf with a very powerful special operations capability. Although the activities of these forces are necessarily shrouded in secrecy, there is ample evidence that they were used extensively and effectively in a variety of missions during the war.

Principal units with a special operations capability deployed to the gulf were the 75th Infantry Regiment (Ranger), the 5th Special Forces Group, the Air Force Special Operations Force, and several Navy SEAL (Sea, Air, Land) teams. Of these, the largest and most capable special operations unit was the 5th Special Forces Group.

Originally activated in the 1960s and used to reinforce the 7th Special Forces Group in the Republic of Vietnam, the 5th SFG has long since assumed responsibility for special operations in the Middle East. The group is extremely strong, with over 50 "A-teams," and personnel have a much higher familiarity with the terrain, language, and local customs than was the case during the Vietnam War. Every team reportedly has a majority of Arabic-speakers, often fluent in the exact tribal dialects of the areas they have trained to operate in.

5th SFG's operational detachments (A-teams, each with 12 to 14 officers and men) are organized in nine companies, which in turn are grouped in three battalions. Each battalion was given the task of supporting one main resistance group: the Kuwaiti resistance, the Kurdish resistance, and the non-Kurdish Iraqi resistance. Each company was assigned to support a particular faction within each resistance movement.

For example, there are three known major factions in the Kurdish resistance: the Kurdish Democratic Party, the Kurdish Workers' Party, and the Patriotic Union of Kurdistan. It appears that each of these had one company assigned to support its operations.

Immediately upon initiation of hostilities on January 16, elements of the II and III Battalions, 5th Special Forces Group, were inserted deep behind enemy lines and began carrying out a variety of clandestine missions. These were a mix of mission types, including support for the indigenous resistance, long-range recon, and active sabotage and combat missions. Most of these remain obscured, but word of a few have filtered out.

- On January 16, a 5th SFG A-team, in cooperation with an Army Apache helicopter gunship unit, destroyed two Iraqi air defense command centers, disrupting interceptor operations and anti-aircraft fire during the critical first wave of air attacks.

- Shortly after the outbreak of hostilities, Operational Detachment A-544 (of A Company, II Battalion, 5th SFG) conducted a HALO (high-altitude, low-opening) parachute insertion behind Iraqi lines and carried out an unknown mission of some importance. One Medal of Honor citation, the first of Desert Storm, is pending as a result.

- Special operations forces were used throughout the war to conduct rescue missions of downed flyers behind Iraqi lines. The first such successful mission was executed on January 21, when a downed US Navy pilot was rescued. The

---

SPECIAL FORCES GLOBAL RESPONSIBILITIES
1st Special Forces Group (SFG): Far East
3rd SFG: Africa (including North Africa)
5th SFG: Middle East
7th SFG: Central and South America
19th SFG: Europe
Special Contingency Global Response: Reserve

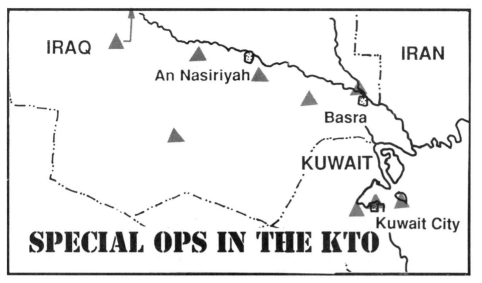

SPECIAL OPS IN THE KTO

rescue force spent at least four hours behind Iraqi lines, both on the ground and in transit through enemy airspace. This mission included members of the Air Force Special Operations Force, and may have been directed by them.

● On January 31, an AC-130 Spectre gunship, flying in support of a 5th SFG operation, was lost behind enemy lines with its full crew of 14.

● Numerous A-teams from 5th SFG were inserted on deep strategic reconnaissance missions along the Euphrates Valley and provided accurate information as to Iraqi movement of reserves and the location of deep defenses. This information was vital to the later rapid drive to the Euphrates by XVIII Airborne Corps.

● Special Forces A-teams operated in cooperation with Kuwait ground forces and Kuwait resistance, and participated in the liberation of Kuwait City. Persistent Iraqi reports of parachute landings west of Kuwait City may have been the result of Special Forces insertions.

● With the ground campaign drawing to a close and the remnants of the Republican Guard penned up against the Euphrates River at Basra, the only escape route left was across the river. Air strikes damaged or destroyed most of the bridges, but commando-style demolition raids by Special Forces teams finished off all that remained, thus sealing the trap.

Throughout the war against Iraq, special operations forces were used boldly and imaginatively. The full range of special operations missions was undertaken and executed successfully. Although a detailed examination of these missions will have to wait for more information, there is no question that the United States demonstrated a tremendously effective capability in this area.

5TH SPECIAL FORCES GROUP DESERT STORM ORDER OF BATTLE

First Battalion
Company A
Operational Detachments
A511 through A516
Company B
Operational Detachments
A521 through A526
Company C
Operational Detachments
A531 through A536

Second Battalion
Company A
Operational Detachments
A541 through A546
Company B
Operational Detachments
A551 through A556
Company C
Operational Detachments
A561 through A566

Third Battalion
Company A
Operational Detachments
A571 through A576
Company B
Operational Detachments
A581 through A586
Company C
Operational Detachments
A591 through A596

DAVID AND GOLIATH
SCUD VS. PATRIOT

The people of London were in terror. People would not go to work, there was mass panic, the war effort was suffering. At the root of the panic was a feeling of hopelessness—nothing could stop the Zeppelins.

Almost 80 years later, few remember the Zeppelin's brief reign as the ultimate invincible weapon. Far fewer people died during the World War I bombings of London then during the World War II "blitz," yet panic was far greater. Much of the explanation appears to be that until higher-flying aircraft, and especially incendiary bullets, became available the Zeppelins really were invincible. Fear seems to run highest when people can't fight back against a threat.

In that vein, the success of the Patriot antimissile system over the Iraqi-modified, Soviet-built Scud ballistic missile was a victory over fear—not just in Israel and Saudi Arabia, but worldwide. Since early in the Cold War, the world has lived in fear of not only atomic weapons, but also of the unstoppable ballistic missiles that carried them. The Patriot has replaced that fear with hope. Unfortunately, a close examination shows the ballistic missile will not become obsolete quite as quickly as the Scud.

THE HISTORY
OF THE IRAQI "SCUD"

Somehow, a NATO code word stuck for an Iraqi-modified Soviet missile. In 1965 the Soviets began deploying an improved version of their SS-1 "Scud," they called the new version "Scud-B." During the 1970s, Iraq obtained a great deal of military equipment from the Soviet Union, including the Scud-B. During the Iran-Iraq War, the Iraqis rebuilt their Scuds in order to reach Teheran. Iraq was quite proud of its missile program, and named its constructions the Al Hussein and the Al Abbas. However, the increase in range made an inaccurate system worse and required a reduction in the size of the warhead:

Scud Versions

Missile	Range (in Miles)	Warhead (in Pounds)
Scud-B	110-180	2200
Al Hussein	375-400	420
Al Abbas	435-550	300

THE ELUSIVE SCUD

The Scud derived most of its effectiveness from its basing flexibility. While the Iraqi Air Force needed long, easy-to-identify runways to operate, a Scud launcher could literally be anywhere. Specially built Scud launcher shelters increased their survivability further. The shelters were simple, vehicle-sized trenches with overhead cover in the middle and camouflage netting over ramps at each end. They weren't much to look at and did not cost a lot, but a great many were built. Even when Coalition pilots found one of the shelters, chances were it was empty.

THE HISTORY
OF THE PATRIOT

The Patriot was not always a hero. Designed to be the US Army's air defense system of the 1970s, development stretched into 1980, over-budget and behind schedule. By 1993, the Army's patience

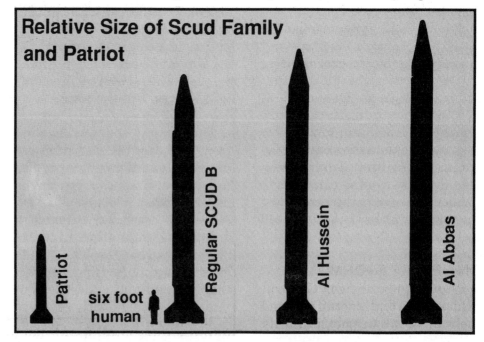

Relative Size of Scud Family and Patriot

Patriot

six foot human

Regular SCUD B

Al Hussein

Al Abbas

seemed to be paying off as costs dropped and production rose. By then, the increasing accuracy of new Soviet tactical ballistic missiles were becoming a concern. In 1984, the US Army initiated a $140 million effort to see if the Patriot could also be made effective against such missiles. The first test of an antiballistic Patriot missile took place in 1987; the first production antiballistic Patriot missile was delivered in September 1990.

WHY THE PATRIOT WORKED

The Patriot worked because it got to the Scuds before the Scuds got to their targets. That's a lot harder than it sounds. Scuds approach their targets at speeds well above that of sound. First, the Patriot's radar must see the missile. The Scud is fairly small, so the radar may not see it at extreme range. When the radar does see the incoming missile, it passes the order to shoot to a Patriot missile automatically; there is no danger of a friendly incoming missile. Then it is purely a race between missiles.

Even a successful interception is likely to result in debris and possibly damage in the target area. By the time of intercept, the Scud has built up quite a bit of momentum toward its target. It's a little like the TV/movie situation where the hero shoots at a car trying to run him over. The hero may disable the driver of the car, but the momentum continues to carry the car toward our hero.

THE IMPACT ON DESERT STORM

Prior to hostilities, General Schwarzkopf and his staff believed the Scud threat was not militarily significant. It is easy to understand why. If one of the Iraqi Air Force's 10 new Su-24 Fencers had managed to take off and reach its target, it would have dropped bombs equivalent to the warheads of 60 Al Abbas Scuds. It may have been his only mistake of the campaign. As the death toll from the Scud that got through days before the end of the war illustrates, US troops staying in tents and temporary facilities were vulnerable to even small warheads. Five hundred American troops were located where one of the first Scud attacks would have hit if the Patriot had not intercepted.

The Scud's biggest impact was in the effort expended to track them down. It was politically necessary to stop Scud attacks, so many sorties were diverted from other targets. The Scuds succeeded in doing what diplomatic maneuvering could not—they delayed the beginning of the ground offensive by several days.

IMPLICATIONS FOR THE FUTURE

The battle of the missiles may have implications beyond our current comprehension. Clearly, the ballistic missile is not obsolete—yet. The Scud was an easy target.

A bastardized version of a 1950s missile, its warhead stayed attached to the missile body, presenting a radar return the Patriot could see relatively far away, thus allowing it more time to intercept. An intercontinental ballistic missile would be traveling far faster than a Scud, giving the Patriot only a small fraction of the time to react.

However, it is clearly feasible to make major improvements to the Patriot. (Simply putting the system in a high-flying aircraft would allow the radar to see the missile farther away and the Patriot to intercept farther away from the target.) Perhaps the analogy to the demise of the Zeppelin menace is incorrect. In the skies of the Middle East we may have witnessed an event more akin to the battle between the *Monitor* and the *Merrimac*—the first skirmish in a entirely new type of war.

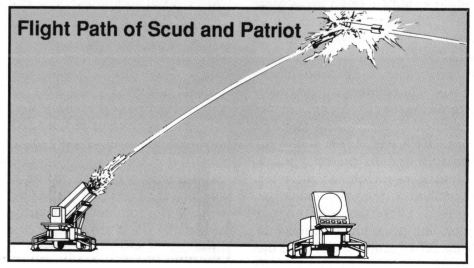

Flight Path of Scud and Patriot

THE WEAPON THAT WASN'T THERE
CHEMICAL WARFARE

Certainly one of the burning questions of the Gulf War was why the Iraqis did not use chemical weapons against the Coalition ground forces. Less than a week before the commencement of the ground offensive, the author was asked during an interview to state his judgment of the likelihood of their use: 80% was the reply. The author was not alone in this assessment: General Schwarzkopf labeled it a near certainty, as did nearly every analyst asked for an opinion.

How were so many people wrong? Why did the Iraqis not use chemical weapons? It is too early to say with absolute confidence, but several persuasive reasons have been put forward. In all likelihood, the correct answer is a combination of some or all of the following.

BAD GAS

When asked why the Iraqis did not use gas, General Schwarzkopf replied that he could not say for sure. When asked to speculate, he offered the possible explanation that the Iraqi chemical agents had deteriorated over time in the shells. The bombing offensive concentrated on knocking out the chemical plants within the first days of the war, and so had eliminated the Iraqis' ability to manufacture replacement chemical agents.

While nerve agents do not deteriorate that quickly, mustard gas does, and mustard gas was the most important chemical agent (from the point of view of quantity) in the Iraqi arsenal.

BAD WEATHER

Chemicals work best in moderate temperatures, low winds, and clear weather. During much of the attack, especially the critical phase after the Iraqis might have begun to figure out the attack, but before their artillery had been overrun, the weather was atrocious. Rain and high winds are very poor conditions for the use of gas; artillery units which could actually identify targets would have been much more effective firing conventional high-explosive rounds.

NO TARGETS

By the time the attack started, the Iraqis had already lost over half of their artillery systems. The collateral damage at battalion and brigade level must have crippled the fire direction centers of many of the surviving guns. Losses in the front lines probably killed many of the FOs for the units still capable of processing fire orders, and the communication links of many of the surviving FOs were probably broken. Field radios tend to be battery powered, and critical daily resupply items for forward-deployed troops are radio batteries.

If the supply system was paralyzed by the bombing, the supply of batteries probably dried up, reducing FOs to using land-line field telephones. By the time of the attack, the artillery and air bombardment had probably broken 80% or more of these land lines. In all likelihood, the FOs would never have been able to identify and engage a target with chemical artillery rounds even if they had wanted to.

NO DESIRE

General Maurice Schmitt, the French commander in chief, reported that Iraqi front-line commanders actually received the order to use chemical weapons from Saddam Hussein, but had deliberately ignored it. His explanation why was that the Coalition had waged an effective PsyOps campaign against their use. Leaflets informed every gunner that individuals who participated in the firing of chemical rounds would be sought out and prosecuted for war crimes, regardless of where they went or how long it took. They even cited recent trials of German World War II concentration camp guards as examples of the lengths the Allies were willing to go to bring war criminals to justice.

This campaign clearly had an impact on the attitude of Iraqi officers and men. By the time chemicals could be used, most felt that the war was already lost, and that using them would only cause their own personal downfall.

If this explanation is true, it is extremely interesting. The troops who had the most experience with chemical warfare, and were best equipped to conduct it, were the

CHEMICAL WEAPONS

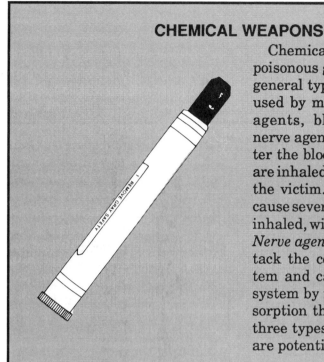

Chemical weapons refer to poisonous gas. There are three general types of poisonous gas used by military forces: blood agents, blister agents, and nerve agents. *Blood agents* enter the bloodstream after they are inhaled and literally poison the victim. *Blister agents* will cause severe skin lesions and, if inhaled, will damage the lungs. *Nerve agents* (or nerve gas) attack the central nervous system and can either enter the system by inhalation or by absorption through the skin. All three types of chemical agents are potentially lethal.

Republican Guard. If those troops deliberately disobeyed Saddam's order to use gas, it speaks volumes about the extent to which Iraqi Army morale and loyalty to Saddam had been eroded by mid-February.

SCUDS AND GAS

The Iraqis never used a chemical warhead on their Scud missiles. This may have been for humanitarian reasons, but a far more persuasive explanation is that they simply never were able to perfect a working chemical warhead for the missile.

What's so hard about a chemical warhead, anyway? Why not just fill the nosecone up with gas and fire the missile? Because when the missile slams into the ground at faster than the speed of sound, it will blow up, and the explosion will burn up much of the chemical agent and drive most of the rest into the ground from the force of impact. The result will be dangerous, but more on the order of a toxic spill than a weapon.

To get the warhead to work, it has to release the gas as it streaks toward the ground, causing an aerosol cloud that will settle over the target. If it releases the gas too soon, it will simply blow away, dispersing over a wide area in non-lethal concentrations. If it releases it too late—boom.

Artillery shells are able to do this. Why not just use the same device on a Scud? The artillery shell's proximity fuse isn't perfect, but it's close enough for something going the speed of a shell. But a Scud approaches the ground at about *twice* the speed of an artillery shell, which means that what are acceptable tolerances in an artillery fuse either scatter the gas at high altitude or slam in into the ground with the missile.

This is not an impossible problem to solve, but it is technically very difficult. Apparently the Iraqis never did manage to overcome it, for which a great many people are certainly thankful.

MOPP Suit

AFTER THE STORM
APPRAISAL

On November 5, 1757, the Prussian Army of Frederick the Great, with a few more than 20,000 men, met a French and allied army of about twice that number in a battle now known as Rossbach. By the end of the day, the French Army had been completely routed, losing 6000 men, for a Prussian cost of only 548.

On September 19, 1415, the English Army of Henry V, with about 6000 men, met a French army of 25,000 at Agincourt, and inflicted a stunning defeat. The French lost nearly half their army (over 10,000 men), versus very minor casualties to the English.

In June of 1967, the Israeli Defense Forces launched a preemptive strike against a gathering alliance of three Arab nations. On the ground, the Israelis were outnumbered 328,000 to 250,000, and in tanks 2330 to 1000. In the air the odds were even more lopsided: 682 Arab combat aircraft versus 286 Israeli. But by launching early strikes at the Arab air forces on the ground, the Israelis were able to gain air superiority, which enabled them to drive home their attacks on the ground with brutal effectiveness. By the end of the aptly named Six Day War, the Israelis had inflicted nearly 18,000 casualties, and destroyed almost 1000 tanks and 450 aircraft. Their own losses had been 5500 casualties, 400 tanks, and 40 aircraft.

Rossbach, Agincourt, and the Six Day War rank as three of the most lopsided victories in military history,

but all of them pale by comparison to the scope and margin of victory gained by the combined forces of the Coalition in Operation Desert Storm. An army of 500,000 men was crushed at a cost of fewer than 100 lives. A force of over 40 divisions, with 4000 tanks, was completely destroyed for a loss of fewer than 10 tanks. Coalition front-line fatalities in the ground portion of the campaign worked out to less than one man killed per enemy *division* destroyed.

It is likely that staff colleges will study Desert Storm in detail for generations to come. For the rest of us, a complete understanding of the reality of this war may prove elusive. When attempting to understand an event, we turn to history for guidance—but history provides few parallels. The only recent battle which seems to approach it in its degree of success was the British campaign against the Italian 10th Army in North Africa in 1940. There, an army of 100,000 simply disintegrated once the forward positions were breached; the roads were choked with soldiers trying to surrender, and the ratio of captors to captives often dipped as low as 1:1000.

But even if cold facts and past incidents can be dredged up to explain away the uniqueness of this victory, the almost otherworldly images and feel of the ground war will remain. The picture of US Marines moving forward under a smoke-blackened sky, the near horizon studded with

burning wellheads spaced at geometric intervals, will always remain with the author. I suspect that it will remain with many of the readers as well.

HOW DID IT HAPPEN?
All events have explanations. The trick is in understanding them. Attempts to explain the success of Desert Storm will draw on a number sources, and it is worth examining them briefly here.

Air Power is Vital
If the enemy controls the skies, you fight blind. If you are blind, you cannot stop a mobile attack. Why? Because mobility allows one side to concentrate virtually unlimited combat power at any point of the line desired, and you can't interfere with that if you can't see it happening. The effectiveness of aerial bombardment in the war has tended to overshadow the critical effect air control has on military intelligence.

Leadership Is Vital
Lopsided victories occur when one side is very smart and the other side is very stupid. The US plan was brilliant; Saddam's stupidity was nearly as important.

Coalition forces were led by experienced and professional leaders from top to bottom. The men and women of the Coalition forces counted on their leaders, and their leaders didn't let them down. When an organization, military or otherwise, has dynamic, assertive leadership, it can perform miracles.

Iraqi leadership, on the other hand, was apallingly bad. All of its best leaders had been purged and replaced by yes-men. Saddam's leadership was catastrophically incompetent throughout the crisis and war. The Iraqi Army fought its heart out against Iran for eight years; its reward was to be hung out to dry by its leadership—an entire field army sacrificed on the altar of one man's ego.

Motivation Is Vital

The Iraqis fought hard for eight years against Iran. In 100 hours, a field army of half a million men threw in the towel. Admittedly, they had been subjected to five weeks of the most intense bombing campaign in history. They had suffered catastrophic casualties, and many units were on the verge of physical collapse due to the lack of food and medical attention.

But not every unit had been decimated by bombing. At least one battalion surrendered to the Egyptian Army with over 700 men and a dozen officers, including the lieutenant colonel in command. This is effectively full strength. Not all of the units were starving; the US 1st Infantry Division cleared bunker complexes loaded with canned goods. Units which were still strong, both physically and in numbers, threw in the towel. Why?

In the Iran-Iraq War, the soldiers were fighting for their country, and under officers who seemed to care about their welfare. In Kuwait, they were fighting to protect stolen property, and under officers who had seen little action in the earlier war and who, in many cases, deserted them as soon as things got rough.

Motivation is closely linked to loyalty, and loyalty only works when it works both ways. As poor a showing as the Iraqi Army appeared to put in, it was infinitely better than its leaders deserved.

Equipment Is Important

The evidence is too compelling for anyone to deny this. The evidence of precision aerial bombing's effectiveness may have permanently changed the balance of forces in the world. Modern Coalition tanks were able to consistently outfight Iraqi vehicles in every category. Stealth technology has revolutionized the air offensive. The list goes on and on.

Troops Are More Important

Good troops can overcome mediocre equipment; mediocre troops can screw up good equipment. The combination of the best troops with the best equipment was unstoppable.

Experience Isn't Enough

The Iraqi armed forces had extensive experience of warfare. They had just brought an eight-year war with Iran to a successful conclusion. The Coalition troops, on the other hand, were largely inexperienced. Britain had fought the Falklands War with marines and paratroopers; this war was fought with tanks and mechanized infantry instead. The Syrians had fought within the last decade in Lebanon, but the 9th Division had not been involved. The Egyptians had last fought a war in 1973, shortly after the US had wound down its involvement in Vietnam. Of the gulf states, only the Omani Army had anything approaching extensive combat experience.

The armies of the Coalition which had fought 10 and 20 years earlier had combat-experienced officers at battalion level and

above, which was certainly an advantage, but their line troopers were almost completely innocent of combat.

One reason that the Iraqis' experience did them little good was that it was the wrong kind of experience. They had plenty of experience in fighting a positional war of attrition. Instead of helping, this was a positive disadvantage when fighting a mobile campaign; they would have been better off starting fresh without a lot of bad habits.

Realistic Training Is Essential

Most aspects of US preparations for war have been vindicated. Certainly the most important of these is training. Our troops performed like veterans, because in a strange way, they *were* veterans. US training has become so realistic that it is able to duplicate every situation encountered in combat except the numbing fear of death. Even fear can be kept at arm's length if the soldier knows what he is supposed to do and has confidence in his ability to do it.

Realistic training can provide this. The Navy's Top Gun program, the Air Force's Red Flag, and the Army's National Training Center pit students against tough, trained opposing forces in extremely realistic maneuvers. Students emerge as veterans. The proof was there to see in Desert Storm.

A NOTE ON SOURCES

In a project such as this, it is impossible to fully credit the many sources drawn on. Heavy use has been made of the various wire services and network reports for the course of events. As time passes, a clearer view of the order and tempo with which events unfolded in the ground war will certainly emerge. This account is complicated by the lag between the time a reporter witnesses an event and the time at which he is finally able to file a story, but the authors feel fairly confident that it is correct in its important particulars.

The hardest part of a retrospective history such as this is confirming friendly and opposing force orders of battle. While hostilities are raging, this is material of an obviously sensitive nature, and must be closely guarded. The Coalition forces, and the United States Central Command in particular, have been extraordinarily forthcoming with such material once hostilities had ceased, and a special debt of gratitude is owed there.

While any errors in judgment or reporting are exclusively the responsibility of the authors, this book would not be nearly so complete or authoritative were it not for the contributions made by a number of people who gave freely of their time and expertise. You know who you are. Thank you.

Readers who are interested in additional reading on the subject will soon be able to chose from an avalanche of books on the subject. Nevertheless, the authors would suggest three possible publications which are definitely worth looking into.

The Air Campaign: Planning For Combat. Colonel John A. Warden III, USAF. National Defense University Press, 1988.

This book is really the first comprehensive attempt at discussing the air war in the context of operational art, and as such it probably represents as import a milestone in US air war doctrine as the first air/land battle documents did for ground doctrine.

It is also a very readable book. Warden understands, as have the most powerful military thinkers of history, that the secret of military art lies in seeing the problem in its simplest terms, not its most complex. The book becomes especially significant due to Warden's involvement in the planning of the air campaign against Iraq. If Saddam had read this book, and understood its implications, he might have thought twice about crossing the line.

Dragons At War: Land Battle In The Desert. Captain Daniel P. Bolger, USA. Ivy Books, 1986. ISBN 0-8041-0899-4.

How were US soldiers, marines, and airmen who had never heard a shot fired in anger able to enter battle with the confidence of veterans? Bolger's book will go a long way to answer that question, and in a very entertaining format. This is a book about combat, but not lethal combat. It is the story of one mechanized battalion's experiences at the National Training Center (NTC) at Fort Irwin, California.

In the course of the book, the author also manages a creditable, but highly readable, coverage of Soviet tactics and equipment, US doctrine, and the highly realistic training programs used by the Air Force's Red Flag project, the Navy's Top Gun school, and the Army's NTC. These programs run troops through real combat—as real as you can get without blood being spilled—and the troops emerge as veterans.

After you read this, you'll understand the comment of a soldier in the middle of the ground campaign in Iraq: "It's not as hard as our training."

For Your Eyes Only. Tiger Publications, PO Box 8759 Amarillo, TX 79114-8759.

One of the most important single sources consulted for background on the buildup of forces and their capabilities was *For Your Eyes Only*, accurately described by its publisher as "An Open Intelligence Summary of Current Military Affairs." It is edited by Stephen V. Cole and published biweekly.

For those with an ongoing interest in military affairs, there is not another single source periodical, to the knowledge of the authors, which contains so much timely, interesting, and useful information.

A one-year (26 issues) subscription is $60 for US, APO, FPO, and Canadian addresses ($32.50 for six months/13 issues). Foreign subscriptions are $77/year airmail (please remit in US funds). Sample copies are $2.00 each. Add 6.25% sales tax in Texas.

Neither GDW nor either of the authors are affiliated with Tiger Publications in any way, and have received no compensation for this endorsement, which makes it as honest a plug as you are likely to find. GDW accepts no liability for subscriptions.

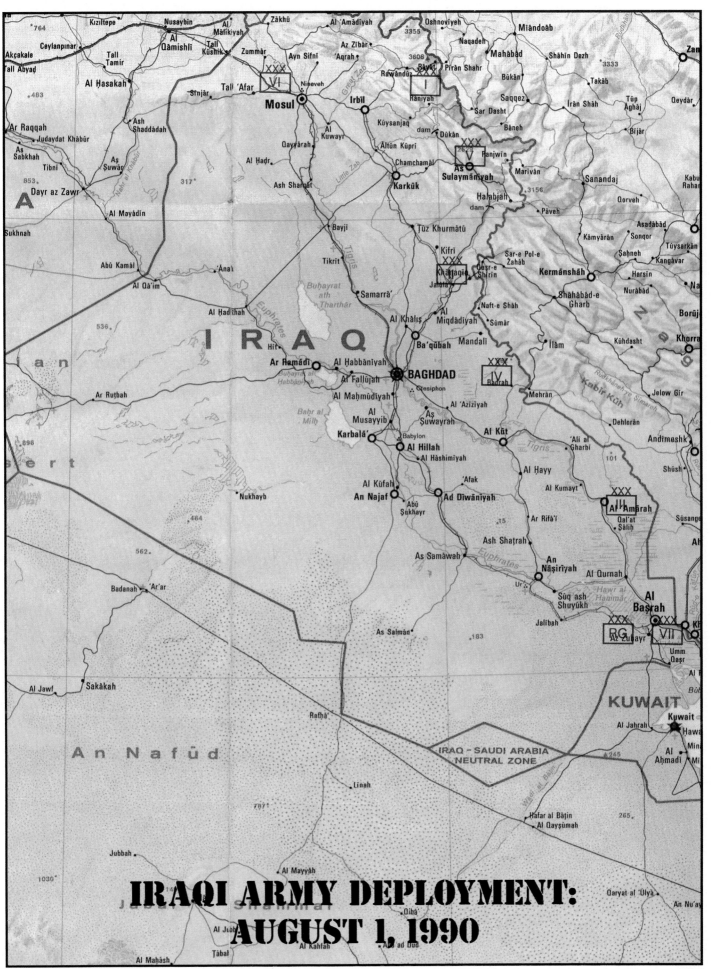

IRAQI ARMY DEPLOYMENT:
AUGUST 1, 1990

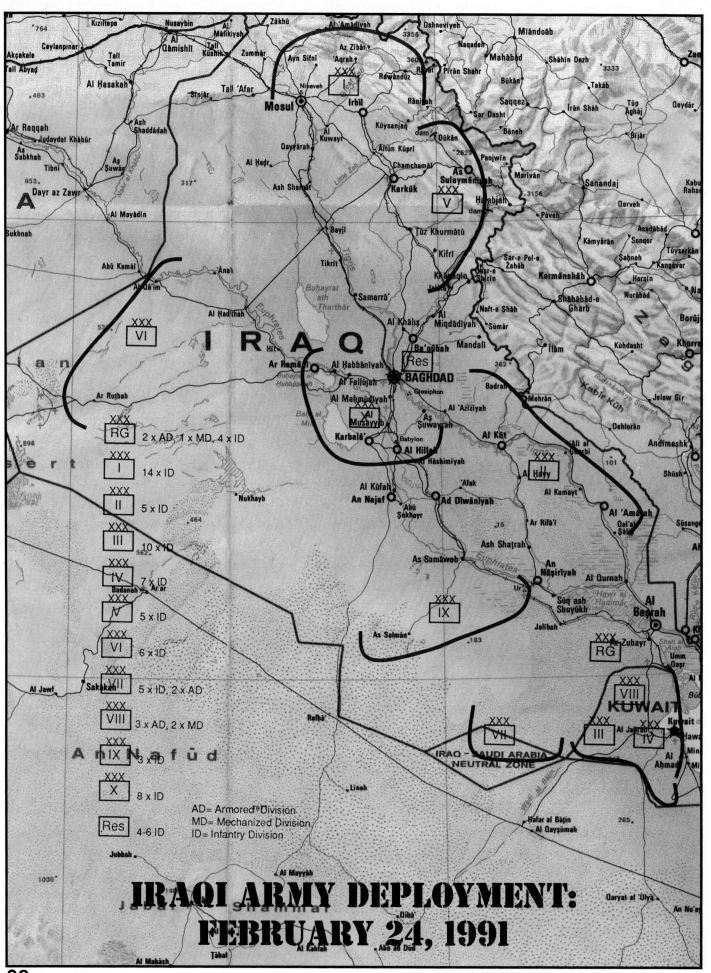

IRAQI ARMY DEPLOYMENT: FEBRUARY 24, 1991

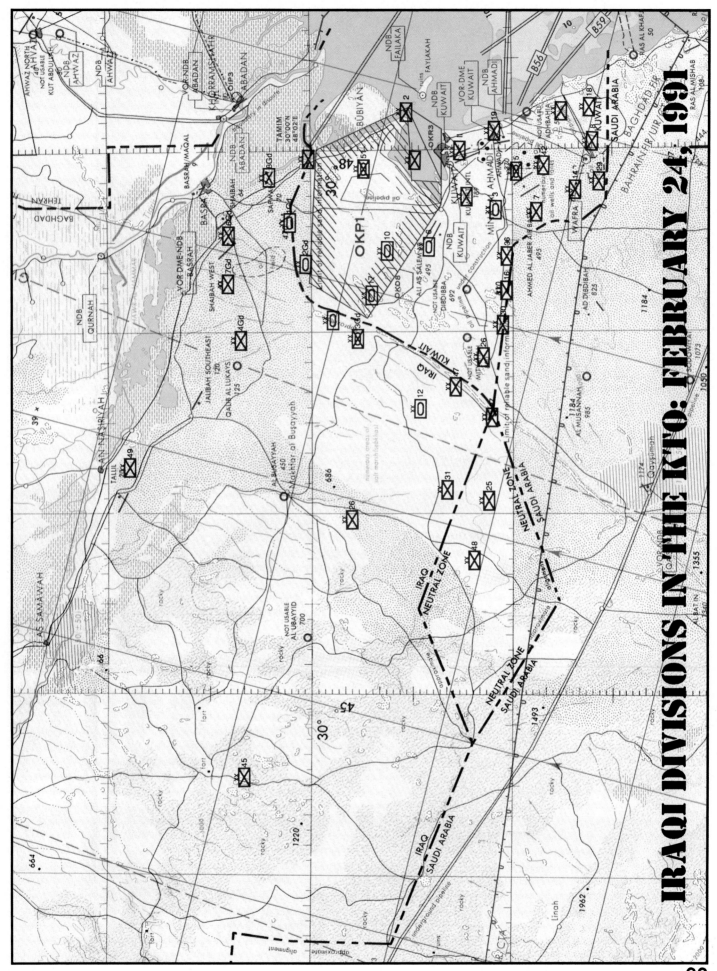

IRAQI DIVISIONS IN THE KTO: FEBRUARY 24, 1991

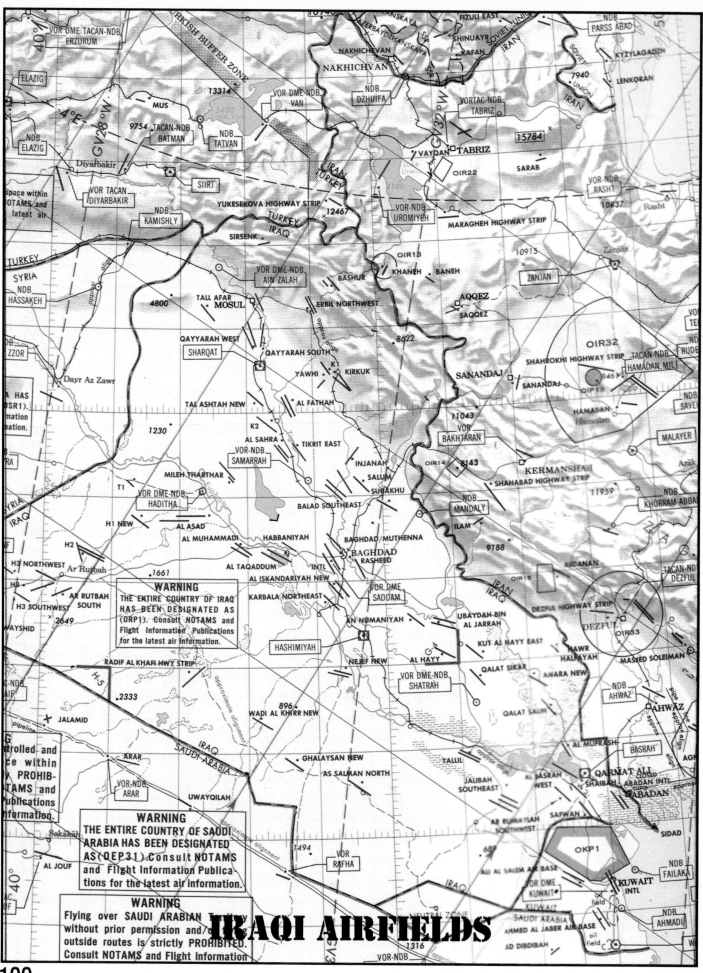

IRAQI AIRFIELDS

100

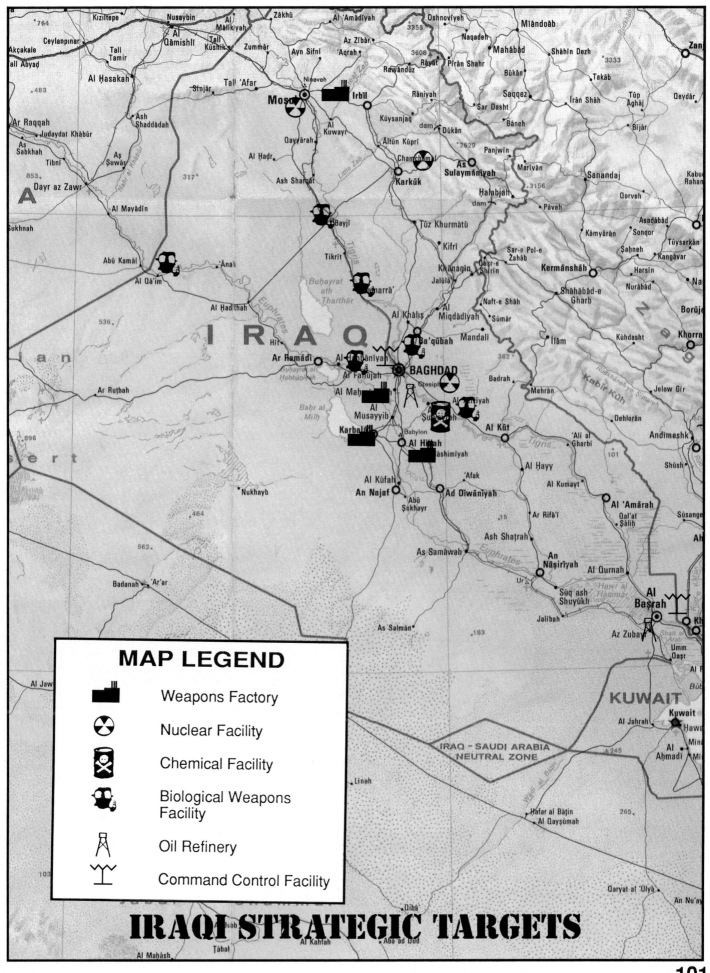

MAP LEGEND

🏭 Weapons Factory

☢ Nuclear Facility

☠ Chemical Facility

☣ Biological Weapons Facility

⊥ Oil Refinery

⊻ Command Control Facility

IRAQI STRATEGIC TARGETS

101

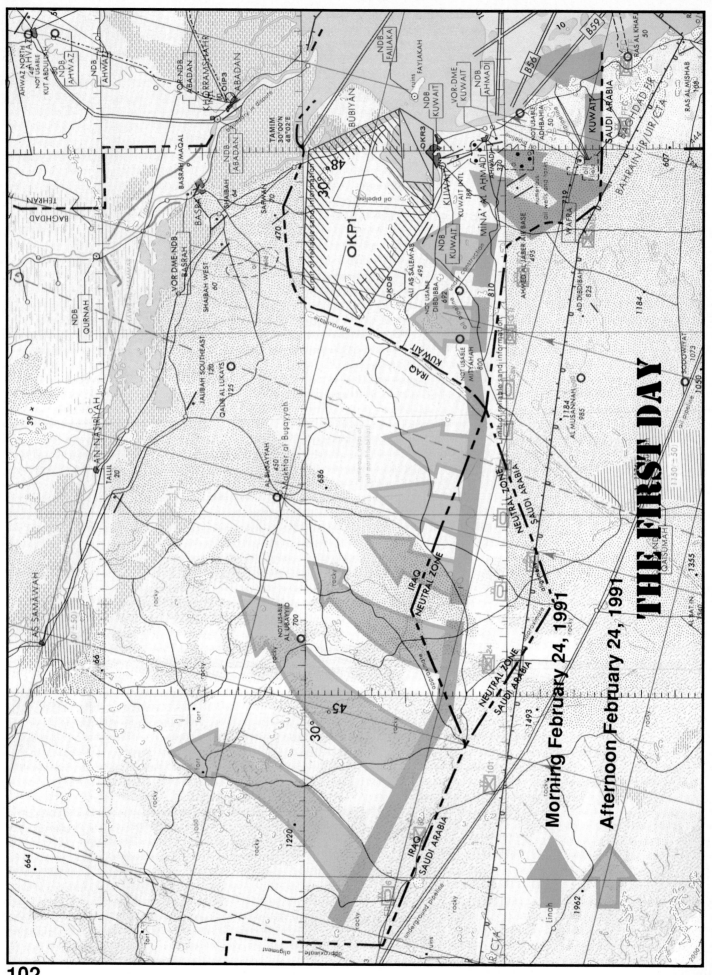

THE FIRST DAY

Morning February 24, 1991

Afternoon February 24, 1991

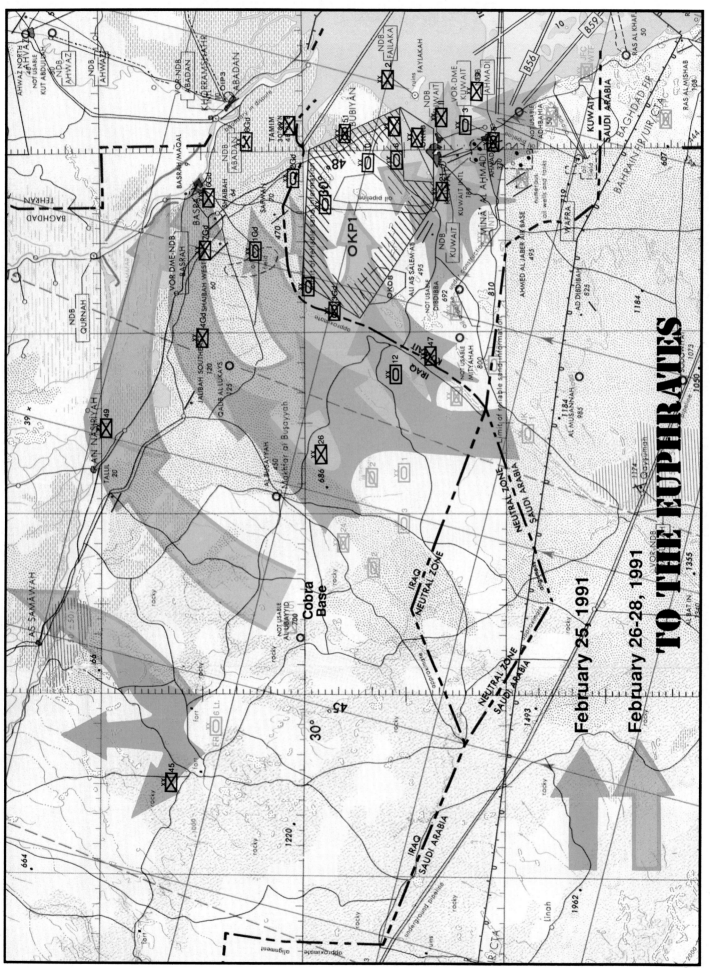

TO THE EUPHRATES

February 25, 1991

February 26-28, 1991

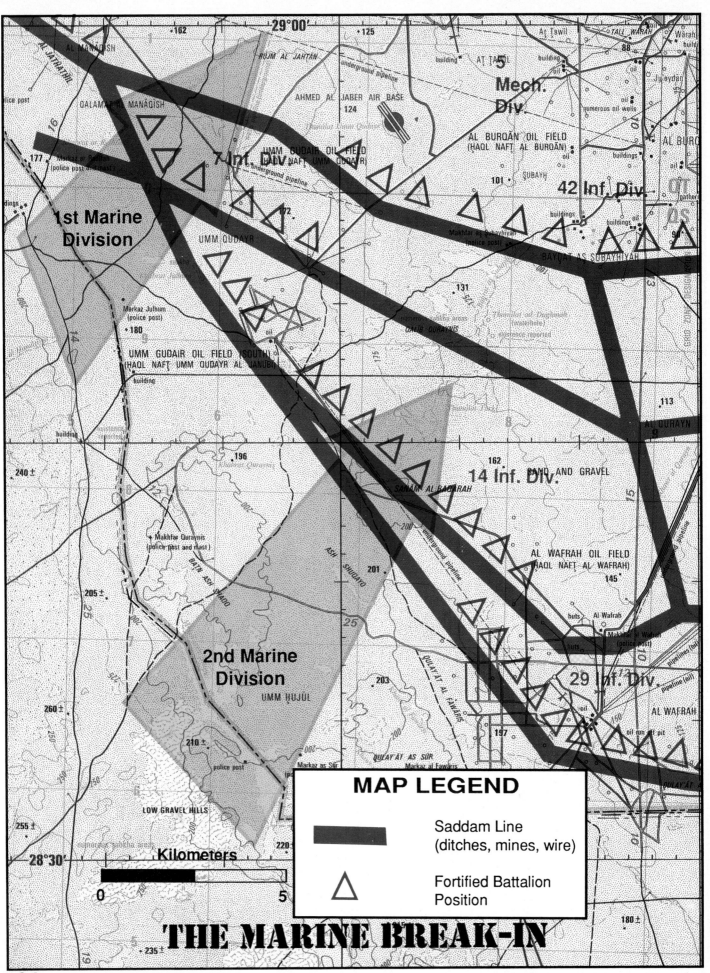

THE MARINE BREAK-IN

MAP LEGEND

— Saddam Line (ditches, mines, wire)

△ Fortified Battalion Position

1st Marine Division

2nd Marine Division

7 Inf. Div.

42 Inf. Div.

5 Mech. Div.

14 Inf. Div.

29 Inf. Div.

Kilometers
0   5